A Teen Marriage Circus

Ghost Pregnancy

Abraham Robinson

ISBN 979-8-88851-739-0 (Paperback)
ISBN 979-8-88851-740-6 (Digital)

Copyright © 2023 Abraham Robinson
All rights reserved
First Edition

All rights reserved. No part of this publication may be reproduced, distributed, or transmitted in any form or by any means, including photocopying, recording, or other electronic or mechanical methods without the prior written permission of the publisher. For permission requests, solicit the publisher via the address below.

Covenant Books
11661 Hwy 707
Murrells Inlet, SC 29576
www.covenantbooks.com

To protect the integrity of the characters in this narrative, we will create a platform that includes a list of character names corresponding to their relationship with the author. For this report, we will refer to this family as the Hatfield's, ensuring the correct names are used for the author and his family as they were at the greatest risk.

1. Father-in-law: Frankie Lee Hatfield
2. Mother-in-law: Kizzy Mae Hatfield
3. Brother-in-law: Bobby Joe Hatfield
4. Brother-in-law: Mickey Joe Hatfield
5. Brother-in-law: Billy Joe Hatfield
6. Estranged wife and daughter of the Hatfield's: Helen Mae Hatfield
7. Granddaughter (Helen Mae and Abraham's daughter): Genoria Mae Robinson
8. Granddaughter (Helen Mae and Charles's daughter): Lillie Mae Robinson
9. Grandson (Lillie Mae's son): John Wayne Robinson
10. Grandson (Genoria Mae's son): David Lee Robinson
11. Grandson (Lillie Mae's son): Frank Wayne
12. Granddaughter (Lillie Mae's daughter): Mae Mae Wayne
13. Grandson (Genoria Mae's son): Buster Smith
14. Granddaughter (Genoria Mae's daughter): Sally Smith

This is a true story about a teen marriage orchestrated by my former mother-in-law, Kizzy Mae, who looked for a way out from her rebellious fourteen-year-old daughter, whom she transferred onto me at the early age of seventeen, which turned out to be the biggest mistake of my life. This changed the trajectory of my quest to attend Jacksonville State University and participate in the school's ROTC program, with the intent of becoming a military officer and reaching self-actualization. As I will demonstrate in this publication, hopefully, I could create a platform that will allow teenagers or young adults who are contemplating marriage to make the best possible decision and to avoid mistakes that can create a lifetime of detriments and financial phenomena that may lead to a trail of human misery and degradation while understanding the importance of selecting the right person from the onset.

Let us begin with my story, the author's background, by providing an insight into my childhood upbringing leading to adulthood and the detrimental effects that have haunted me ever since joining this circus marriage.

My name is Abraham Robinson. I was born in January 1957 to James Lee and Bessie Pearl Robinson of Birmingham, Alabama, during the time when Dwight D. Eisenhower was the 34th president of the United States of America. As a result of this loving and stable union, this marriage produced six siblings, starting with Leroy, James Jr., Wilbur, Abraham, Victor Lee, and Jimmie Louis, also known as the Robinson boys.

Although my father, a native of Columbiana in Shelby County, Alabama, and mother, a native of Birmingham in Jefferson County of the same state, moved to Birmingham after serving in the United States Navy, which my father would always joke about his classification as a Seabee (a construction worker) and that he would say to the departing sailors, "See you when you leave, and be here when you get back," his mother—my grandmother, Hixie Mae Robinson (Tatum)—would inform him while he was serving in the military about a house for sale located at 1406 Sixth Avenue North that was vacant, instructing him to send a portion of his earnings so she could purchase this house and to make available when he's discharged from the service. My father was a proud World War II veteran serving at Okinawa, Japan, among other military assignments. That house was where I was born and raised until I relocated to Pascagoula, Mississippi, after graduating from high school because of Kizzy Mae and Helen Mae's deceitful phenomenon, and Jerry's life-changing phone call that exacerbated this whole ordeal!

In that home, I learned what a loving and cohesive family was all about. Growing up with five brothers and no sisters paved the way for me to learn how to keep the house as my mother was very adamant about cleaning and ensuring that we understood the importance of candor and integrity, as well as cooking and the basics of homemaking, including the importance of cleanliness. In fact, my beloved mother would always leave money on a dresser in plain sight to instruct her boys about the importance of not touching money just because it was present unless it was intended for us. As a result of this early childhood training, the concept of candor and integrity became paramount, paving the way for life clear of the judiciary system.

As a craftsman and builder, my dad instilled in us the importance of learning how to repair automobiles, plumbing, masonry, construction of homes, and other skills that have proven to be beneficiary many years later. He would always say that I must learn and become intellectual and should not rely on things that were on paper only as a method to know how to comprehend what is important or necessary while completing a task. Interestingly, this revelation came true when I was stationed at Fort Drum, New York, the tenth mountain division, and assigned as a switchboard operator and when I was tasked to deploy to Fort Ord, which is now closed, as a special tactical satellite radio operator during training to operate this radio. I took excellent notes and relied on the notes but was unable to find the notes when I needed them, which led me to be dropped from this special deployment that I was excited about attending. This confirmed my dad's advice about not relying on notes on paper as I experienced this firsthand as described above.

In fact, my father would give us one dollar a week as an allowance, showing us how to save money and purchase items at an early age. This was an experience that my life was very enjoyable and rewarding as I would make sure that my behavior was always positive to continue to receive that incentive. On the contrary, my mother did not give us cash directly but would purchase things like clothes, food, and other necessities that were paramount to our survivor, including demonstrating how spouses should work in unison. One of the things I would do with my dollar–per week allowance was to save for the spring season to purchase vegetable seeds for planting, which my mother was fascinated about as she mentioned years later.

I started my academic journey at the early age of three. I enrolled in a neighborhood childcare worker head start home school, which was operated by an older lady we called Ms. Nanny. Matter of fact, I can still remember the first song she taught us, which went something like this: "The line starts at the state store door, up the alley the way they go, they drink wine, gin, and whiskey too while stagging right down eight avenues." She lived on this avenue for the record. Moreover, the childcare worker interactions prepared me to enter grade school with the knowledge of understanding my ABCs and the bases of numerical numbers, as well as interacting with my peers, which subsequently established a platform for a high school diploma, associate degree in prelaw, bachelor's degree in political science, master's degree in business administration, and a doctorial learner of performance psychology.

After completing my head start, my parents enrolled me into the local grade school named Lincoln Elementary, where my mother was employed as a custodian worker, thus opening various doors where I was recruited by the legendary Dr. Frank Adams Sr., a Birmingham jazz all-time great saxophone player and influential teacher. He was acquaintance with my mother as she would ensure that the school was clean and sanitized so the children could learn and study in a safe environment that mitigated various anomalies and diseases. As a result of my mother's reputation as an excellent employee who loved children and their wellbeing, I was recruited by Dr. Frank Adams Sr. He introduced me to a musical instrument called the saxophone, which I played in the marching band and over the next five years.

I did not continue playing this instrument after graduation due to my phobia of joining the Parker High School band, which had a reputation for bullies and gangsters. One Friday afternoon, when I was a first-year student, while preparing to go home, I was approached by a senior with a beard named Craig. He said to me, "I guess you know by now that I do not like you."

I was shocked by his feeling because I did not know he was observing or stalking me. So I calmly closed my wall locker door and walked away, not showing any indication of fear toward him, as I was briefed earlier about the reputation of the high school for having bullies and gangsters.

Nevertheless, my parents enrolled me at Parker High School, which I was zoned in to attend. While attending Parker, I was considered a ringleader of good morale and, in most classes, considered a top student among my peers and instructors. An example of one of my mathematics instructors was when she gave the class a diagnostic test to check our skill levels, and I earned a grade of 100 percent. She then immediately moved me to a more advanced class in algebra, where I had to make new friends all over again, which is something that I regret to this day. And if I would have known that earning a grade of 100 would have been the cause of my transfer away from my established friends, I would have failed it on purpose.

One day, during woodworks class during my senior year, a junior student named Bobby Joe approached and started a conversation, which subsequently led to a friendship with me, since I was an easy-going guy who just wanted to enjoy the moment and welcome anyone who had a good sense of humor and ability to have a good relationship with me and since I was considered a class clown who enjoyed inducing a smile and laughter from other students.

As a student, I played on the school football B-team and participated in many other school activities, such as welding, joining the debate team and the student government, where I served as the class president. I was invited by Bobby Joe to his home located in the western part of town one day and met his mother who offered me dinner, which I accepted. An invitation that set the stage for the circus to originate turned out to be the worst experience imaginable.

As a motorcycle and automobile owner with part-time employment after school and a person from a stable home with both parents, his sister Helen Mae began to say that I was her boyfriend. Matter of fact, she was infatuated with me and always insisted again that I was her boyfriend so much that her mother began to say that she's gone "Abraham crazy" every day whenever I came over with her brother Bobby Joe. She was very persistent and adamant about developing a relationship with me even though I did not know her or even had any feelings toward her, which never changed during the entire tumultuous relationship.

One of the things that concerned me about Helen Mae was the argumentized relationship she had with her father and brother Mickey Joe. They cursed each other every time I was present. Interestingly, I have learned from this experience that a woman who has issues with her father and brother is most likely to have problems with her husband or boyfriend as was the case in this tumultuous relationship.

In fact, her father warned me and stated that something was wrong with that girl. This advice later proved to be beyond reproach. Additionally, it was appalling the way Helen Mae wore a rag tied around her head like the slave women of the 1800s and the way she straddled the family dog across her right shoulder as though she was carrying an infant, as well as driving her to her psychologist office and picking her up four hours later. I could not hold her father responsible for any of her behavior there as he warned me in advance, giving me the opportunity to reconsider and vacate any idea of having a relationship that ruined my life!

But her mother, Kizzy Mae, on the contrary, was looking out for her by selecting a partner for Helen Mae that had what it took to provide a financial and stable environment, from which I came, which she was right! She also realized that Helen Mae was destined to get pregnant anyway and produce children out of wedlock as did her brothers and subsequently Genoria Mae and Lillie Mae as we are going to elaborate on later in the manuscript.

So I began to attend the football and basketball games and hang out with Helen Mae and after school study to increase our vocabulary with various lists of words obtained from my homework—something that she appeared to enjoy until her brother Mickey Joe would constantly criticize her for enhancing her knowledge base.

After dating Helen Mae for only six months, I had the premonition to author several poems concerning our relationship and had them copywritten with the United States patent and copyright office. The titles of the poems were "Anyone Can Turn a Doorknob" and "Lover Needs Your Guarantee," which proved in many ways to fit our relationship. In that Helen Mae's loyalty to other men and the fact that I needed her guarantee to be someone that I could be proud of were themes that never materialized even to this day. Additionally, I retrieved two albums from her trash can, one titled *Lover Need Your Guarantee* and the other *Oh, What Fun We Families Will Have When Santa Claus Arrives on Christmas*, which were inadvertently damaged by someone using a nail or some pointed object to scratch across the vinyl, rendering them useless.

Moreover, I took it upon myself to enhance her vocabulary and teach her how to drive a car although she was not old enough to obtain her driver's license due to her age. Three months away from leaving to attend Jacksonville State University, her mother, Kizzy Mae, informed me that Helen Mae was pregnant in January 1975. I was only seventeen years old, inexperienced, and had no clue about marriage whatsoever. I passed a handwritten rough draft copy for a wedding invite to be carried to my mother that evening when I left their home.

When I gave my mother the notice, her advice was "Men do not marry women just because they are pregnant. They marry for love and a long-term relationship." I was oblivious to this fact, and as a churchgoer, I thought it was God's will for me to marry to prevent childbirth without divine intervention through marriage. So I disregarded my mother's advice and made one of the worst decisions in my life, with the second worst decision coming when my so-called best friend called informing me about a job opportunity in Pascagoula,

A TEEN MARRIAGE CIRCUS

Mississippi, as I was prepared and set to attend Jacksonville State University located in Jacksonville, Alabama.

My mother informed me that she was not going to participate in any marriage concerning a fifteen-year-old girl and stated that if Helen Mae were her daughter, she would not approve of it. Now faced with the birth of a child, which I had no clue took about nine to ten months, I decided to go ahead and marry her and prepare for the birth, based on Kizzy Mae and Helen Mae's announcement of the pregnancy in January 1975.

Many years later, my mother referred to the forty-fourth US president, Barack Obama, and his wife, Michelle, as an example of two people with similar goals that paved the way for a successful career. In that, she recommended going forward to always select a woman who has the same admiration as myself. In her words, "Get someone who wants something and is willing to work together." This advice was obviously too late as I had made one of the worst mistakes in my life—being associated with the Hatfield family. However, I have adopted this advice as a catalyst going forward with future relationships.

Interestingly, the first president that I voted for was the thirty-ninth US president, Jimmy Carter, who during his last television interview celebrating his seventy-fifth wedding anniversary with his wife Rosalynn was asked what it took to make their marriage have such longevity. He said, "Number one, you have to pick the right person." Now from experience, this statement collaborated with my mother and her girlfriends' advice concerning the compatibility between me and Helen Mae, which was tested the first night during our honeymoon that was a disaster—a day I wish I could forget!

Moreover, she subsequently gave birth nineteen months or about a year and a half later, which discerned the ghost pregnancy phenomenon, where she either believed that she was pregnant in January 1975 and not giving birth at the appropriate time or she became the first woman to give birth in nineteen months, thus paving the way for her to enter the Guinness Book of World Records.

Because of this deceit, I was compelled to seek employment and abandoned my quest to attend Jacksonville State University and sought a career as a military officer in the US Army and subsequently a career as a politician. Therefore, I was compelled to accept a position at Ingall Shipyard in Pascagoula, Mississippi, as a welder, despite better the judgment recommended by my best friend, Jerry, who later accompanied Helen Mae on a secret dinner date without my knowledge and approval.

I found out about this date when Helen Mae would brag about how Jerry was a better man than me because he was wining and dining with her while I was at work. In fact, he would always laugh at every joke and comment that I made during our high school years. After taking Helen Mae on their secret dinner date, one day, he told me about his brother who was serving time in prison for a felony and how he wished he was out. I told him that if his brother did not commit the crime, he would not have been there in the first place!

He became extremely irate, jumped into my face in front of my wife, Helen Mae, and began to yell at me, cursing me out, which was appalling as I did not know that this behavior was part of his character. He then began to stop speaking to me even though he was the one who called asking me to accompany him on this job at the shipyard. Now we were still sharing the same apartment, with him not speaking to me but speaking to my wife, which I thought was strange and unacceptable.

Moreover, Helen Mae's mother, Kizzy Mae, set the marriage date for November 1975, giving me time to secure a job and prepare for a journey that turned out to be the beginning of the marriage circus. To ensure that I would return to marry her daughter, she authorized her son Billy Joe to accompany me to Pascagoula, where he was able to report back to her and escort me back to marry his sister.

During our commute back to Alabama, one of our vehicles began overheating, resulting in us being more than four hours late for the wedding, which caused most of the attendees to leave with the impression that I did not want to get married. In retrospect, in my mind, this was divine intervention letting me know that my mother and her friends were correct, and I should not have participated in this circus marriage. In fact, if her brother was not present, I would have left her standing at the altar as I had a change of mind!

A TEEN MARRIAGE CIRCUS

Interestingly, I have learned from experience that if any of your parents, without cause, decides not to attend your marriage ceremony, as I did with my mother, one should step back and reevaluate the situation, which was something I failed to comprehend due to immaturity on my part and not listening to my mother.

My dad was the type of father who supported me even if I was wrong but would correct any behavior that could cause me or anyone else harm. Although he was unaware of the mastermind behind the decision to marry Helen Mae, it was done by Kizzy Mae at her request. This supported the theory that Helen Mae was pregnant in January 1975, which was inaccurate and disgraceful.

When we finally arrived at my church, Zion Hill Baptist, we then got married. During our honeymoon, Helen Mae was truly angry about my tardiness that she did not allow me to touch her or even communicate with her and made me realize that I had made a serious and life-changing mistake! In fact, we had started a discussion about annulment, thus considering the dissolution of our marriage after only one hour of being married.

All the signs were there that Helen Mae and her mother's arranged marriage was a serious mistake. In hindsight, allowing her mother to propose to me for her was inappropriate, and it should have been me to ask Helen Mae for her hand in matrimony.

Looking back, the only time that Helen Mae and I kissed was during our wedding ceremony and never again since. I refer to that kiss as one for the ages since it was the last time our faces were that close together. One of the reasons was I did not know her or had any loving feelings toward her. In today's life terminology, she would or could have been considered a friend with benefits, which would have been a safe and effective way to get to know her and discover that she was not pregnant in January 1975 as indicated by her mother. In other words, if I had known that Kizzy Mae and Helen Mae were not being truthful about her pregnancy, I would have left her and never looked back!

Before marrying Helen Mae, she had met with my mother's girlfriend, Rosie Mae. After spending a day with Helen Mae and interviewing her, Rosie Mae emphasized that we were not compatible, which I later found out to be the truth, the whole truth, and nothing but the truth. After Helen Mae met my other family members and friends, they all said that she was not compatible with me and that someday I would find it out for myself, which I did in a dramatic fashion that still haunts me even to this day. And as a release mechanism, I had to write this publication to share with others the torment that I endured that affected me and hope it will aid someone else not to make the same mistake.

Interestingly, the female neighborhood that I had grown up with and witnessed this circus marriage was very disappointed in me for giving Helen Mae the opportunity that they thought should have gone to someone that I knew from early childhood and my neighborhood. In fact, many years after our marriage had ended, I had refused other women who wanted to marry me from other parts of the world because of what I had learned from the women that I had grown up with and not giving them the opportunity to experience a partner that understood the value of having a good partner and one who had the privilege to grow up with both parents in the home and one who was employed and did not count on public assistance because of their ambition to get out of poverty.

For the record, any woman that I grew up with and met around the world, including France, Germany, Belgium, Panama, Costa Rica, Honduras, El Salvador, Canada, Egypt, and Israel, would have been a better choice than someone like Helen Mae, whom I have never known even to this day, some forty-six years later. She used to brag about having sex with other men as if it were a joke, all while being married to me. It is something that I will never forget as long as I am mentally healthy and possess the cognitive skills to discern the difference.

A male acquaintance named Delvin told me after interviewing Helen Mae after the wedding that she informed him that the only reason she got married in the first place was to rid herself of her mother Kizzy Mae and to get out of the house. While I appreciated this information, I informed this acquaintance that during the wedding and before the pastor announced that we were married, he said, "Speak now or forever hold your peace." He became angry with this statement as I informed him that if he did not say anything about Helen Mae then, then he did not need to say anything now.

Moreover, after returning to Pascagoula, as mentioned earlier, I later learned that my friend Jerry was taking Helen Mae to dinner without my consent. This revelation was revealed when Helen Mae began to brag about her dinner date with Jerry and how he would take care of her while I was at work each night. Interestingly, he kept this secret and did not mention it even to this date. Oh, and Jerry had two sisters that were not allowed to communicate with me. I noticed one night he became irate when he noticed that his sister and I were talking on their front porch. He began to yell and shout out, "Everybody trying to talk to my sisters, now you are trying to talk to them. You are supposed to be my friend!" I was shocked and just proceeded to my vehicle and left his neighbor as though nothing had happened while making sure to communicate with his sisters when he was not available for safety reasons.

One night, during my tenure at Ingall Shipyard, I slipped on an iron beam and was sent home to recuperate. When I returned home unannounced and opened the door, Helen Mae and a foe of mine named Maurice jumped off the couch, looking startled. Although I was appalled, nevertheless, I walked past them and went to bed. Twenty minutes later, Helen Mae entered the bedroom, not saying anything, and went to sleep.

Several days later, she disappeared and returned to Birmingham while I was at work. Because of Helen Mae's immaturity and relationship with Maurice and Jerry, her abrupt return home perpetuated my decision to return to Birmingham and continue my academic endeavor at the University of Alabama, which was derailed by Kizzy Mae and Helen Mae earlier with my intent to attend Jacksonville State University. I was also employed by Caldwell Foundry as a second-class welder, subsequently passing the company-required testing through Pittsburg laboratory, earning the status of a first-class welder, and becoming the company's first African American to hold such a position.

Now Helen Mae began to show her pregnancy around April 1976 again, but it never dawned on me that her mother's announcement about her pregnancy in January 1975 timeline should have been completed by then if she was pregnant in January 1975 as stated. She later gave birth in August 1976 to a baby girl (Genoria Mae), who they raised in such a faction and became alienated at an early age that we had not spoken for forty years and still have limited contact even to this day, some forty-six years later.

In fact, Genoria Mae is raising her children in the same fashion as her mother Helen Mae and grandmother Kizzy Mae taught her regarding having limited or no communication with me or the Robinson family, which I have no regrets about as life goes on and the same thing applies to Genoria Mae and to her children. In that, they will lose more not knowing me than me not knowing them. Interestingly, her husband's side of the family, the Smiths, did not experience the same phenomena.

In fact, one day, I was out cutting my mother's grass when a stranger pulled up in his car, stopped, and informed me that the boy, Buster Smith, who was in the car was my grandson. I immediately went inside and informed my mother of this unorthodox encounter with a stranger who had to inform me that I had a grandson, which supported the concept of Kizzy Mae and Helen Mae that raising Genoria Mae, who never had anything to say or do with me or the Robinson family even to this day some forty-six years later, was groomed after their behavior pattern.

In fact, Kizzy Mae gave our daughter their name that I did not approve of and regret even to this day. Kizzy Mae has passed away now. And because of our toxic relationship and her entrapment that led to me marrying the worst woman that I have ever seen worldwide, I could not attend her funeral.

When Helen Mae gave birth in August 1976, it came time to leave the hospital. The administrators refused to give Genoria Mae to her because of her age. She called me from my work and informed me that they would not give the baby to her. So I clocked out and went to the hospital, and as soon as I turned the corner to the nurse's station and without identifying myself, they immediately, without any hesitation, handed me the baby and I gave her to Helen Mae and returned to work.

A TEEN MARRIAGE CIRCUS

Unfortunately, we cannot turn back the hands of time. If we could, I would have left Genoria Mae in the hospital, requiring Kizzy Mae to get her or bound her over to the state social services department for adoption.

Again, I gave the baby to Helen Mae since she had a way back to her mother's residence. Ironically, she returned to her mother's residence and began to curse me out and call me various names without cause because she wanted her mother to raise our daughter without any input from me, which perpetuated a breakdown in the relationship with me and Genoria Mae's life, to the point when she got married, many years later, I didn't attend her wedding and wouldn't sign off on it because of her behavior toward me and my family.

In fact, her uncle Bobby Joe had to become her father that day and walk her down the aisle. At the time, I was over at my best friend's home partying with some elderly women and informed them that Genoria Mae was getting married that day. Then with an inquisitive look on their faces, one asked, "Why are you not at your daughter's wedding?" I explained that Genoria Mae and I did not speak and that she had the same attitude toward me as Kizzy Mae and Helen Mae did and I was not going to tolerate this type of behavior from a daughter who had never referred to me as her dad. In fact, I thought she had autism because she never spoke in my presence and acted strangely.

Although Genoria Mae did not need my signature, unlike her mother who was fifteen years old at the time of her marriage and needed her parents' signature to marry at an early age, Genoria Mae was old enough to sign her own signature for marriage. In addition, the wedding did not cost me one penny, as was the case with Helen Mae's family who paid the entire cost.

In fact, Kizzy Mae arranged for me to pick up my dad and Helen Mae's father, Frankie Lee, who warned me in advance that his daughter had mental issues, which I failed to understand until we got married and only found out on the first day during our so-called honeymoon. We went to the courthouse and filed and signed the marriage paper, paving the way for the wedding to take place.

Interestingly, many years later, I found out that Helen Mae had no clue that her mother had arranged for this transaction to take place.

Moreover, Genoria Mae did not understand the repercussion that her behavior would have in the future, which prevented me from supporting her marriage to the point where when she was facing her own divorce, she called me and said her husband wanted a divorce and she did not. I informed her that I did not blame him because she had been raised by Kizzy Mae and Helen Mae and her values did not align with her husband anymore, causing a breakdown in their marriage.

After our conversation, Genoria Mae called her mother, who called me immediately and asked why I was acknowledging that Genoria Mae's now estranged husband was doing the right thing. I informed Helen Mae during the conversation that Genoria Mae and her husband, Buster Jr., were from unusual backgrounds. Genoria Mae grew up without a father and came from government housing supported by child support and other government aid, while Buster Jr. came from a loving home with both parents in his life, where his father was employed and had a supporting spouse that understood the importance of teamwork.

After their wedding, his father came by my mother's home where I was residing and informed me that he thought it was strange and unusual for the father of the bride to not be present at his only daughter's wedding. I informed him that Genoria Mae and I had never spoken since her birth, and she was displaying the same behavior patterns as Kizzy Mae and her mother Helen Mae—something that I was not going to tolerate and did not.

Additionally, Buster Sr. informed me that Helen Mae was unfair and egregious to him and his wife by not giving them a rose and passing by them as if they did not exist. I explained to him that Helen Mae was the worst woman I have ever met. She was someone who had issues with her father and brother Mickey Joe, and she was jealous that Buster Jr., the groom, had his family support, unlike Genoria Mae who did not have the support of her father as I did with mine. I also informed him that Helen Mae's wedding with me was a disaster and this was her way to show how displeased she was that his son had a successful event.

After returning home from the hospital, Helen Mae resided with her mother and dated a man named Charles, who was the potential father of her second child named Lillie Mae. To cover her tracks, she had never lived with me or even visited the home that I had prepared for the new arrival. In fact, I had to ensure that the home was equipped with hot water, bedding, a refrigerator, etc. to pass an inspection from the department of human resource services, which we did. Yet Helen Mae never spent one night at the apartment I had provided since leaving the hospital and cursing me out the same night without cause.

To give the relationship another opportunity to strive, I suggested that we move into a luxury apartment, which she agreed to but only lived there for seven days. During her brief stay, here's what transpired, on the second day of being employed at the Caldwell Foundry as a welder, my vehicle would not start because of battery issues, so I decided to call the bank where Helen Mae was employed to ask her to come home during her lunch break so I could get a boost off from our other vehicle, so I could be on time for my second shift work assignment. When I called her office, I was told that Helen Mae had called in earlier, reporting she was sick. She had scheduled a date with a new boyfriend, which was something that was routine during our entire tumultuous and unimaginable relationship that was established by her mother.

On the fifth day, which was her day off, I noticed that as soon as I prepared to leave the apartment for the evening shift, the first thing she did was change her regular pants to her favorite short Daisy Dukes–style hot pants and left as I was backing out of the driveway, heading somewhere. I assumed she was heading to Kizzy Mae's public housing but not positive since she lacked integrity throughout our entire relationship. On the sixth day, she and I went and rented a shampooer so she could clean the carpet while I was working that late evening because she was complaining about the carpet. When I left and went to work during my late lunch break, I decided to drop by unannounced to check on her progress with cleaning the carpet, and here's what happened: She had goofed off the entire afternoon, and within two hours of my work shift to end, she and Kizzy Mae were over there, trying to finish the carpet that they had recently started as I noticed due to the distance of the carpet being clean, which was about 10 percent completion. On the same day, I learned that she could not operate an electric range since her mother only used gas in their public housing, which was something that could explain why she would bring food home from Kizzy Mae's residence. On the seventh day, I noticed that she had vacated the apartment and returned to public housing, a place that she was familiar with and had raised Genoria Mae and Lillie Mae for most of their lives.

Let's back up to the first apartment for a moment. So one Saturday night, out of nowhere, Helen Mae knocked on the door, entered the first apartment, and insisted that we have a brief intimate encounter, which I found strange because this was the first time she had visited the new apartment and voluntarily requested to have an intimate relationship with me, which I accommodated and then she immediately jumped up and left the apartment and never visited that apartment again. Her actions left me battler because the last time we had spoken was when she was cursing me out and being very disrespectful, calling me names and hanging the phone up in my face, as well as taunting me about how other men could have sex with her any time. They felt like it while I could not, and we were married at that time.

She subsequently gave birth to Lillie Mae in June 1977, which was approximately ten months after the birth of her first daughter. When I questioned Helena Mae about the validity of this birth, considering she was residing with her mother and dating Charles at the time, her comment was, "It doesn't matter if you are not the biological father because we are married, and this child was caught up in the web." The court would oblige me to pay child support since my name was on the birth certificate, and I need to get over it and learn to live with the notion of having a child that could be another man's. She informed me that I could not prove otherwise since I had not witnessed her having an intimate relationship with Charles. I accepted this narrative since I did not know anything about having a right to know if we had the same DNA.

One day, without prior notice, I abruptly visited Helena Mae since I was laid off for two weeks due to tardiness. I inspected what was going on with her and met her boyfriend Charles, who had purchased some hair products for his daughter, Lillie Mae, who was born during the time Helen Mae was stilled married to me. He became extremely angry when I took the bag of hair products and returned them to him.

Although I felt like he was her father, not to mention that they looked more alike than me, I knew Helen Mae and I was still married. He could not admit that he was the father of a child that was born while Helen Mae was married to another man. This would have put Kizzy Mae and Helen Mae in limbo and start a new court battle, requiring them to face charges of adulterous when DNA claims would prove that Lillie Mae was indeed Charles's daughter. This could result in him having to pay child support, which would negate my obligation to another man's child.

Moreover, when I gave Charles his gifts back, which he purchased for his daughter, Lillie Mae, Charles bolted out of the back door, went to his car, retrieved his pistol, and yelled for me to come outside. But I remember something an old white lady for whom I worked during yard work told me to always remember that "a scary chicken who runs gets to live to see another day." So I did not go outside because he would have terminated my life. Now, during this time, Helen Mae encouraged me to go outside, but I refused. She began to curse me out and call me names, such as coward, ugly, black with big lips, etc.

As she displayed an incredibly angry disposition toward me because she knew the truth about her and Charles's relationship that I inadvertently stumbled upon because of my company's unforeseen layoff, I was glad that this occurred. This was like the same experience with Maurice while residing in Pascagoula, Mississippi—an incident that had never been addressed since her abrupt departure from the state.

Moreover, after Charles left in his car, I then left Helen Mae's mother's home and went home but never forgot how close I came to fulfilling Helen Mae's prediction and favorite talking point that someone would terminate my life before the age of twenty-two or be confined in a wheelchair that would require Genoria Mae to serve me water. Her favorite statement was she would teach her children to always hate me and that their father got killed in the army as it was her goal to establish the same tumultuous relationship she had with her father. I must say that Helen Mae accomplished her goals as her children have demonstrated that she taught them well when it came to not interacting with the Robinson family.

How wrong Helen Mae's premonition was in predicting my early demise because I have lived three times. She predicted that I would not live and I would not be in a wheelchair as mentioned earlier. In fact, I have reached the age of sixty-six, healthy as a horse, not in a wheelchair (no one can predict beyond the moment), and I do not need Genoria Mae or Lillie Mae to serve me water as predicted by Helen Mae.

Moreover, Helen Mae demonstrated from day one that she had a greater loyalty to other strange men than what she was providing to her husband at the time. She would always say, "You're just mad because every man can have sex with me but you, and we are married," which was the only time I could definitively say she was being candid. Many years later, when I was serving in the army and Helen Mae was employed by a bank in their data center just before our second divorce, I brought a soldier friend home one weekend and decided to contact Helen Mae to visit her job site and meet my new friend. Guess what happened next? When Helen Mae came downstairs and saw my new friend, Sergeant Conway, the first thing she did was hug me and began to walk with him down the hallway while I was walking just behind them as though I was their friend. But again, Helen Mae had demonstrated repeatedly her disloyalty to me and to my family.

So after I had dodged a potential life-ending ordeal with Charles, I went back to our apartment, where she and our daughter had never resided, to prepare for my night shift as a first-class welder for Caldwell Foundry. Yet because of this tumultuous relationship with Helen Mae, I was laid off again for the second time in two weeks, which allowed me to visit Helen Mae and my daughter Genoria Mae during the daytime. However, I was shocked to learn that she had been dating another guy named Wilbur Gary, who was a friend of her brother Mickey Joe. When this relationship was revealed, I had to accept it at this time because she was living with Kizzy Mae, her mother, and not with me.

One day, I stopped by and witnessed her and Wilbur sitting on her mother's couch. I just turned around and left. It became apparent who Helen Mae was, a promiscuous woman just sewing her oats as the old folks use to say.

So it was Saturday night during my work suspension, and I stopped by again unannounced and noticed that Helen Mae was answering the door, wearing only her red underwear. I reminded her that she was still married to me and that answering the door in her underwear would not be tolerated. She began to yell and curse at me. Kizzy Mae came from the living room and pulled out a Smith and Wesson .22-caliber pistol. She pointed it at me and said that Helen Mae could answer her door in her red underwear if she wanted to and that I need to leave immediately, which I did to prevent Helen Mae's prediction from coming true, concerning my early death. There was no doubt in my mind that Kizzy Mae would have pulled that trigger and killed me and would call the police, informing them of some misleading and concocted narrative to cover her misdeed.

Another incident involving Helen Mae occurred when she was supposed to pick me up from work, but instead, she was out with her brother Bobby Joe and his girlfriend Annette and almost killed our daughter Genoria Mae in a car accident. The car, a 1976 Opel made by Isuzu, was completely totaled in the accident. However, some divine intervention saved their lives as I witnessed the destruction of the vehicle.

I had to walk home and catch a ride over to her mother's home to find out about the accident. Since the car was in my name, my insurance company had to pay the claim. Later, I informed Helen Mae that if she had been where she was supposed to be, this accident would not have occurred, and as usual, she began to curse me out and call me various names.

However, it did have a negative effect on our daughter Genoria Mae as she struggled to take her first step. Her sister Lillie Mae, Charles's daughter, was an inspiration in her taking her first step through observational learning as Lillie Mae began to walk first. This enhanced Genoria Mae's confidence to do the same.

Genoria Mae's progress in walking started when she could not walk at the time. Her sibling, Lillie Mae, had developed a technique that I thought was interesting that allowed them to slide down the stairwell. But when they both started to walk, the first thing they would do when they saw me was to run and leave the room as Kizzy Mae and Helen Mae would giggle at their actions, which I thought was appalling. But when Charles and other men were present, Genoria Mae and Lillie Mae would be sitting on their lap or playing with them.

After her mother Kizzy Mae pulled a gun out on me and Helen Mae's infidelity, I decided to file for a divorce in 1978 and pay child support and give her any property she wanted even though she had never lived in the apartment. She came over with her brother Billy Joe and took items like lamps, television, stereos, and anything that she could pack into the car I had left because of the court order for the convenience of Genoria Mae to commute back and forth to daycare and the doctor's office. So in this case, I was paying for her car note and child support and providing medical insurance that Helen Mae abused to get even with me as we will be discussing later in more detail.

Moreover, during the divorce proceedings, Helen Mae told the judge that she didn't want a divorce from me, and it was me who wanted the divorce. While sitting at the lawyers' table with both lawyers and Helen Mae was sitting in the audience with her mother, her lawyer passed a document to my lawyer Bruce. After reading it, he passed it to me, and I read it and noticed that Kizzy Mae and Helen Mae concocted yet again another false story, stating that they had witnessed me having sex with my daughter Genoria Mae.

A TEEN MARRIAGE CIRCUS

They never mentioned Charles's daughter because when her name came up, I would always remind them about my conviction concerning Charles. One morning before school, I was informing Kizzy Mae, Helen Mae, and Lillie Mae that she was not my biological daughter. She turned toward Kizzy Mae, who informed her that she did not need a father and that her grandmother was all she needed as she giggled. Well, that afternoon, when I stopped by, Kizzy Mae was terribly angry about my comments that morning and informed me that I was not welcome at her home where Genoria Mae was residing and receiving child support. Now I was forced to consider the relationship Kizzy Mae had with her father since she and Helen Mae did not want me to have a relationship with Genoria Mae, as was the case her entire life.

However, the false statements made by Kizzy Mae and Helen Mae concerning an inappropriate relationship with Genoria Mae were emphatically doomed by political endeavors. My goal was to run for lieutenant governor of the great state of Alabama; but out of fear that this would embarrass my immediate family and myself, I had no choice but to scrap my plans to seek the office. I was reminded of what a lady once told me concerning women like Kizzy Mae and Helen Mae. "I must always have a witness present, so if she lies on me, they will also have to lie on my witness."

Attorney Bruce recommended that we do not mention this in court to negate the embarrassment that this revelation could cause me since the court was full of litigants. So my lawyer informed me that Kizzy Mae and Helen Mae were seeking full custody of my child, depriving me of visitation rights and leaving me only responsible for paying child support and providing medical care and transportation, and that I needed to agree to give up my legal and visitation rights for Genoria Mae. I responded by saying, "I do not care if I ever see Genoria Mae again in my lifetime because she was going to miss me being in her life more than her being in mine!"

Before Genoria Mae reached the age of majority, Helen Mae and Kizzy Mae had a change of hearts and story and informed the court to restore my visitation rights, which I did not care about one way or another since she had been alienated and had nothing to say to me for years even today.

Well, the judge asked me if I wanted a divorce or if I would be willing to go back home and work it out with Helen Mae. I responded that I wanted to proceed and terminate the relationship because I was tired of the Hatfield's circus that was run by a mother-in-law, who was not an honest person and even pointed a handgun at me, threatening my life, which is something that I will never forget.

The judge finalized our divorce, ending our tumultuous relationship with me paying the car note, medical bills, child support, splitting the household goods, and not being able to visit Genoria Mae. But on the contrary, the visitation did not apply to Charles's daughter, Lillie Mae. Again, Kizzy Mae and Helen Mae had visited the courthouse and rescinded this order before Genoria Mae turned eighteen because they did not want history to show that they were the cause of father and daughter having an estranged relationship. Also, they did not want to create a platform after she reached the age of majority to tell her that I could not be in her present life because of her grandmother and mother's outrageous claim of incest. They also understood that when Genoria Mae reached the age of majority, she could overrule the court order, terminating the visitation rights. In addition, I showed Helen Mae and Kizzy Mae that life goes on with or without having a relationship Genoria Mae as is the case today.

Today, I considered Genoria Mae as a mama's girl instead of a daddy's girl, and I wish I was not her father and connected to the Hatfield family. However, as soon as the court had adjoined, I immediately went over to Kizzy Mae and Helen Mae's apartment and informed Genoria Mae in their presence that they told the judge that we had an intimate relationship and had slept together. Genoria Mae, embarrassed, responded in their presence by saying, "No, we didn't." However, she made a statement that we will revisit later in the book.

Now after the divorce, Helen Mae began to carry the children to the doctor three to four times a week to create a massive batch of bills, drove by my house without any warning, dropped them off on my front step, got back into the car she acquired during the divorce,

A TEEN MARRIAGE CIRCUS

and spaded off. This action revealed that she was a revengeful, out-of-control person out to get even because of our divorce.

I was leaving for work when I noticed a big brown envelope stuffed with over three hundred bills, ranging from thirty dollars to three hundred dollars. I paid the bills as it added to child support and bolstered her financial dilemma on me. However, I returned to work and developed an invention with a patent number of 284282 and produced two albums and ten copyrighted songs that I decided to table because I did not want to make the Hatfield family a millionaire class of people because of their relationship with the Robinson family and the fact they were not used to such financial status as they sought public assistance for survival.

One day, Genoria Mae developed a devastating rash on her arm while residing with the Hatfields. Kizzy Mae sent Helen Mae back home for the first time to let me see that Genoria Mae had a medical issue, and without hesitation, I immediately took her to the children's hospital emergency room and got the doctor's attention. Then they gave her a shot and an ornament gel that negated the rash.

While we were sitting in the emergency room, Helen Mae and Lillie Mae got into a word argument about me being her father. Lillie Mae began to brag about me being her father. Helen Mae responded by saying, "How do you know if Abraham is your father?" She informed Lillie Mae that she was not present when she was getting pregnant and her claim about me being her father was not true. What Helen Mae failed to realize was making that statement in my presence was going to come back to haunt her even to this day as Lillie Mae and I do not speak and have accepted the fact that I am not her father as she refused to take a DNA test to prove otherwise. In public, she acted like we were not acquainted, pulling up next to me while driving and pretending like we have never seen each other.

Once the doctor took care of Genoria Mae's medical situation, Helen Mae and I returned to Kizzy Mae's apartment, where she was briefed about our emergency room visit while Helen Mae took Genoria Mae back upstairs. On the next day, Helen Mae resumed cursing me out and calling me several types of bad names. Again, this was a way to ensure that her mother raised Genoria Mae as she saw fit, and as a result, Genoria Mae and I have no contact even to this day, some forty-six years later.

One day at work, while on break, I was pondering something that former president John F. Kennedy had said on television about the phrase, "Ask not what your country can do for you but what you can do for your country." This revelation perpetuated me to consider joining the army as I thought about age being a factor and that someday I would be too old. And if I did not go then, then time could pass me by. So I went and joined the army in December 1980 without the knowledge and approval of Kizzy Mae and Helen Mae since we had already divorced. But before I left, I paid off the car, the 1976 Opel, and ordered the finance company to send the title to Helen Mae because she would allow her brother Mickey Joe to drive the vehicle anytime while it was in my name, unaware that I would be responsible for his actions because the insurance company did not have him down as a legal driver and the fact that he did not have the authorization from the owner to operate the vehicle in the first place.

She allowed him to drive while denying me the same opportunity because he would curse her out all the time, so to mitigate their estranged relationship, he could drive anytime he wanted to. And when Mickey Joe had locked the engine up, she called me and told me that I needed to get the car, or she was going to junk it. I retrieved the vehicle and requested the title, but she refused the title, which raised a red flag in my head because of her previous behavior regarding integrity. Although I did retrieve the vehicle and thought about repairing it, I later changed my mind since I knew it would end up being driven by Mickey Joe.

Now after completing base camp at Fort Knox, Kentucky, I was sent to Fort Lee Virginia to advance in school to become an equipment records and parts specialist. I had known of no plan to rekindle a relationship with Helen Mae, Kizzy Mae, or even ever seeing Genoria Mae again in my lifetime, but due to a call from the American Red Cross, who informed me that my father had been hospitalized because of a stroke, I immediately returned home on an emergency leave of absence.

A TEEN MARRIAGE CIRCUS

As I was holding a meeting with my family, one of my brothers yelled out and said that someone was outside blowing their car horn, asking for me. I was shocked and terrified to find out it was Helen Mae of all people. I am still trying to figure out to this day how she found out about my return. However, at the direction and advice of her mother, she took me to the nearest hotel and forced herself onto me and then took me to the courthouse and begged me to remarry her, which I reluctantly did unfortunately.

I did know the mistake that I was making at the time, but I was hoping she had somehow changed as my attention was on my beloved father's hospitalization. So I remarried Helen Mae secretly in 1981 and was too ashamed to let anyone know that I had become a two-time loser or that, in some cases, met the definition of insanity. Once we married, she did not attend the funeral. In fact, that was the last time I saw her until she came to my base at Fort Stewart, where she tricked me into returning home and draining my lifesaving before my military contract was supposed to end and failed to honor her commitment to purchase a new house for us, which perpetuated the reason for our second divorce and a marriage that lasted only half of the day.

While serving at Baumholder, Germany, she was unaware of my location, so I pretended to be stateside and called her, informing her that I was coming over to visit her. Genoria Mae would start yelling and cursing at me, telling me to not come or she would call the police. I found it fascinating since the last time I saw Helen Mae was when my dad was hospitalized, and she insisted that we go to the hotel, which subsequently led to our second marriage.

Several months later, I called from Germany and her brother Billy Joe's girlfriend answered the phone and would not allow me to speak to her, stating that Helen Mae was not my wife or even being married to her at the time. Billy Joe's girlfriend and Helen Mae had been going to nightclubs together, so she may have been exposing infidelity inadvertently. Moreover, twelve months later, my army roommate and I were watching a movie when a mail was delivered. I received a letter from Helen Mae, and I began to open it while my roommates looked on and noticed that Helen Mae had sent me her wedding ring back from our first marriage, which was something that she could have done during our first divorce. After our first divorce, she decided to keep the ring, but the second marriage gave her the opportunity to return the ring to show that Billy Joe's girlfriend, her nightclub friend, was telling the truth when she said Helen Mae was not my wife and that the marriage license was a fraud.

My roommate jumped out of his bed, laughing, and started to run all the way down the hallway, yelling that my wife had another man and returned the ring as proof. Although I had paid thousands of dollars for that ring for our first marriage, I sold it to my roommate for ten dollars that he wore on his pinky finger, mocking me every day until he left Germany. This wedding ring was from our first marriage that she had concealed and I had forgotten about it until she returned it, letting me know that she was dating other men while I was serving my country in the US Army.

While serving in Germany, I worked a second job off-duty at a rod and gun club as a cook and bouncer. This second job allowed me the opportunity to save every penny of my military check and pay my bills without any problems and prepare to become an entrepreneur by starting a general service business with my talented brothers upon completion of my military service, which I was scheduled to transfer back to the United States soon.

As mentioned earlier, Helen Mae would always say that someone was going to take my life and she would tell Genoria Mae that I got killed in the army. Well, her prediction almost came true on the night when I was invited to a going-away party, which was traditional while serving overseas.

While I packed and waited on the bus scheduled to arrive at five o'clock the next morning, I was patiently waiting in my quarters, minding my own business, when I received a knock on my door by a Sargent Taylor, informing me that a going-away party had been arranged for me in another soldier quarters. So I left with him, and when I entered the room, a soldier they referred to as a body man grabbed me from behind and pinned my arms to my side while about ten to twelve soldiers started to kick and hit me, twisting my arm and legs and choking me. But since I took my physical training seriously,

A TEEN MARRIAGE CIRCUS

I was able to move the crowd down toward a bed rail, where I locked my only free hand onto a bed rail. In the meantime, the shortest soldier in the room and possible the ring leader took a pillow off one of the other beds and attempted to suffocate me by attempting to seal the pillow covering my nose, but the bed rail prevented him from getting a good fit. I did not panic as I knew it was imperative that I stay calm until help arrived, which it did after ten minutes of loud noise coming from the room.

After this incident, I retrieved my bags and returned to the bus depot where I waited for the bus. As I pondered this incident, I thought about Helen Mae, who would always say that I was going to die early and predicted that I would not see age twenty-two and that I would die in the army or at the hands of one of her boyfriends and or some unknown stranger.

Her prediction almost came true because I was twenty-three at that time. Again, she would always say that she would tell Genoria Mae that I had been killed in the army, which almost happened that infamous day in Germany, a day I will never forget. Remember, Helen Mae and Kizzy Mae always left Charles's daughter Lillie Mae out of any situation or discussion because they knew who the real father was, and it was not me as they were aware of based on Helen Mae's promiscuous behavior that was imminent from day one of their first meet as discussed earlier in this manuscript.

Upon leaving Germany, I reported to Fort Stewart, Georgia, where I continued to save money and attended college and worked off-duty at the bowling alley as a cook in preparation to become a successful entrepreneur. I received a commander memo warning me that Helen Mae was using the American Red Cross as a personal bank because she was reporting to them, asking for money to pay her bills, which I had to repay through payroll deductions although she was receiving child support through an allotment. I must say that Kizzy Mae and Helen Mae were cunning when it came to pilfering and using government and private agencies for their benefit as was the case with the American Red Cross.

Three months before being discharged from the army at Fort Stewart, Helen Mae called and said she wanted to buy a home for us to live in because she did not want to live with her mother. To reinvigorate this tumultuous relationship concocted by her and her mother, I allowed her to commute to Fort Stewart, and I was shocked and appalled to see her walking down the walkway, asking strange soldiers how to locate me.

As she approached me, she suggested that we go to an off-base hotel where she again forced herself on me and requested me to get a leave pass and return to Birmingham to withdraw my entire saving, which I foolishly did, so she could plan for my return by purchasing a new home. She said everything had been finalized and the only thing she needed was my lifesavings to complete the home purchase. She assured me that she would send the keys to the house in thirty days.

So I returned home and went to the bank, accompanied by Helen Mae. As we conducted the withdrawal transaction, the bank teller recommended she'd place the money into a new account for safekeeping since it was a tremendous amount of money. She giggled just like her mother would customarily do to me and, while doing devious things, informed the teller that she wanted cash only. So the teller acquiesced and began to count out thousands of dollars to her that she placed into a larger lady handbag. She then exited the bank and drove me to the airport for my afternoon departure.

After draining my life savings and returning to the base the same day, I waited for about two months and called Helen Mae and inquired about the house purchase and the door keys. She began to curse me out and said she had children with me and that my lifesaving was for them and then hung the phone up in my face. Interestingly, when I returned to the same bank after discharging from the army, the same teller remembered the transaction and said to me, "Do not let some women make a fool out of you because they will if you let them," which is something I have always remembered some forth-six years later. Moreover, when I informed my mother about the transaction, she said that I should have waited until I was available to purchase the house instead of relying on Helen Mae, who was unemployed, to conduct the house purchase without my input.

A TEEN MARRIAGE CIRCUS

Nevertheless, around thirty days before discharging from the army at Fort Stewart, I contacted Helen Mae again about the new house keys and then she giggled and began to curse me out, calling me various nasty names while informing me again that Genoria Mae and Lillie Mae had decided to not live with a mean man like me, and hung the phone up in my face—something that she would do repeatedly throughout this tumultuous relationship orchestrated by her mother.

In retrospect, we had never spoken on the phone during our brief dating experience, which was a terrible mistake on my part because this ordeal would have alerted me to her lack of communication skills, which became apparent from so many hang-ups whenever I called about the family business.

When I got out of the army in 1984, the first order of business was to file a second divorce and attempted to recover my lifesavings. My brother Wilbur said to me that I gave away the money for the family business. He did not know how bad that made me feel, allowing a person with only a high school education and a mother who pulled a .22-caliber pistol on me and, in retrospect, tricked me the way Helen Mae and Kizzy Mae had done to me over the years.

Moreover, during our second court appearance, the judge asked Helen Mae what she did with my lifesaving. Her response was she bought two cabbage patch dolls. But in fact, she failed to mention that she had purchased a new blue Camero and paid for a wedding with her new husband named Jason Simpkins and subsequently purchased her own home near her mother, Kizzy Mae. Now her relationship and marriage with Jason did not last long because Jason was not going to tolerate Helen Mae with two children displaying the same behavior to him as she did to me. Once she spent my saving with her new husband Jason, he had no reason to continue their relationship.

Unfortunately, I was out with a friend and former coworker, whom everyone referred to as Bad Jasco. He had a notorious reputation with his peers, displaying an angry attitude, especially when he had been drinking, such as what happened that night as we left a nightclub. Some would say a hole in the wall.

Well, our car, a 1976 Cadillac Sedan that I borrowed from my brother, would not start. I informed him that Helen Mae lived nearby. He had met her earlier before our first divorce. But I told him that when we arrived at her door, I would need to stand behind him and let her see his face to enter her home since she had pilfered the money from my saving earlier. I knew she would not open the door for me regardless of an emergency. The plan worked as she looked out of her door and saw Bad Jasco and immediately opened the door. Bad Jasco thought it was amusing as he would tell most of our peers about the door incident.

When Helen Mae opened the door, I began to inform her that Bad Jasco and I had car problems and needed a ride to my brother Wilbur's, also known as Big Moose, home for assistance. Although she had two men sitting on the couch, she said *okay* and left them at her house as though they lived there. As she went into the bedroom to change into something more suitable for travel, I especially informed her that she needed to take Bad Jasco home first as a safety measure since I knew his reputation when it came to women. In fact, he had shot and killed his baby daughter many years later for denying him whiskey. So out of concern about what Helen Mae did that night is something that I will never forget.

Again, after not heeding my warning about Bad Jasco, she took me home first, but what was interesting was that the temperature on this summer night was about 90 degrees and the humidity when she turned on the car heater while I was sitting in the front seat, which made me uncomfortable during our commute to my brother's home to borrow his car.

Although I informed Helen Mae that I could take bad Jasco home in my brother's car, she insisted while giggling that she was going to do so and began to ask me to exit the car. As I began to exit the vehicle, she switched the control from the heater to the air conditioner when she dropped me off as he moved from the back seat to the front seat. Moreover, the night Helen Mae dropped me off first against my recommendation, I decided to mark time for the future to see if they went straight home, and here is what occurred.

A TEEN MARRIAGE CIRCUS

As soon as I got dropped off and exited the vehicle, she switched the dial on the car dashboard from the heater to the air conditioner and pulled off with Bad Jasco. I knocked on my brother's front door and informed him that I needed his car for a little while, and he said *okay* as usual, which empowered me to begin to mark time to see if Helen Mae and Bad Jasco went straight home, and here is what transpired:

I left Big Moose's house and drove to Helen Mae's house first to check if she had arrived, and she had not. Then I drove to Bad Jasco's house and was informed by his wife that he was not at home, then I drove back to Big Moose's house and started the marking process again by going back to Helen Mae's house and noticed that she had not returned as was the case when I went back to Bad Jasco house for a second time and was informed again that he was not at home.

After repeating this process five times and they still had not arrived, I went home and then began to call Bad Jasco until he finally answered the phone and said he just got home. I informed him that I wanted to make sure she had arrived safely. I was marking time that allowed me to formulate a timeline for the future. I did not call Helen Mae because she was not answering the phone when her caller ID showed, it was me calling, which was the reason I had to stand behind Bad Jasco just to get her to open the door in the first place. So to avoid having to answer the question of why she had a new house that was purchased with the money she had tricked me out of during my Fort Stewart assignment, Helen Mae ensured that Genoria Mae and Lillie Mae were living with Kizzy Mae, with little or no supervision.

After that night, Bad Jasco began to refer to Helen Mae as a "much right woman." And when I asked why he referred to my then ex-wife Helen Mae as "a much right woman," he responded by saying that it meant that Helen Mae was just as much his woman as she was mine or any other man's—something that has haunted me for many years. In fact, one day I was joking with him, informing him that Helen Mae and I were contemplating having another child when he said something strange about her reproductive organs and her body scar.

After giving birth to Lillie Mae while still married to me, she underwent surgery without my permission or input, which would prevent her from having any more children. She did not want to become a young woman with six or more children from different fathers, as was the case with Lillie Mae and Genoria Mae who have two different fathers in their lives. Unlike me, I followed the divine route of marrying first before having children.

Moreover, the surgery left a visible horizontal scar that Bad Jasco described to me one night when we were discussing and joking about Helen Mae giving birth to another child. Bad Jasco, with a serious look on his face, said, "You know that Helen Mae cannot have any more children, so why are you joking about her having more children?" What he did not know was he was confirming the notion that I had regarding the night Helen Mae insisted on taking him home first. This provided him an opportunity to make a definitive statement about her ability to have more offspring. The only way Bad Jasco could have known about the horizontal scar was if Helen Mae would have discussed this with him, which would have been inappropriate, or if he had seen it for himself, which would have required her to be undressed, exposing the scar. This was something that the timeline that I conducted that night could have easily revealed.

This experience taught me two things about Helen Mae: she would pilfer and lacked moral candor. From that point on, Bad Jasco would share his experience with Helen Mae that night with his male friends, who would mock me every time they were in our presence. In fact, one guy told me that he knew Helen Mae, referred to her as Boo, and told me that he could take her from me any time he wanted to while sitting at Bad Jasco's kitchen table. Both men giggled while rolling their eyes back and forth.

I informed this clown that Helen Mae was my ex-wife, and her mother Kizzy Mae arranged this marriage to rid herself of an out-of-control and dysfunctional daughter, who became the worst person I have ever met in my life. I informed Bad Jasco that Helen Mae was a divorcée and could date anyone she wanted to.

Now, as a civilian with no money, I had to move in with my family. Helen Mae was very disrespectful toward them and would often refer to my mother by her first and middle name, Bessie Pearl. She even taught Genoria Mae to do the same as reported by my mother while I was serving overseas.

Matter of fact, my mother had put a high school ring for Genoria Mae on layaway, making monthly payments toward it. But when she reported to me that Genoria Mae had been disrespectful to her, referring to her as "Bessie Pearl" while tickling Helen Mae, I reimbursed my mother and informed her that I would finish paying for Genoria Mae's high school ring, which I never did or had any intention of doing.

I informed my mother that I would personally deal with Genoria Mae over the years as we did not speak for forty years. Now Genoria Mae does not want to tangle with me for any reason because she knows that I will put her in the same boat as Kizzy Mae, Helen Mae, and Lillie Mae, as was the case for forty-years. While she should not care about this relationship, considering we had never bonded or lived together, I have always told everyone I met who asked if I had any children that I did not. I was never proud of Genoria Mae or Charles's daughter, Lillie Mae, because of their behavior toward me all their lives while being raised by the Hatfield family.

Interestingly, when comparing Genoria Mae's behavior with that of her stepsister, Lillie Mae, I must admit that Genoria Mae had no clue how to deal with her father as she would stick to Helen Mae and Kizzy Mae like glue. On the contrary, Lillie Mae would constantly laugh, joke, and carry herself as though she was my biological daughter.

But when Lillie Mae reached high school age and gave birth out of wedlock, she became arrogant and sneaky. One night, while I was on active duty at Fort Campbell, Kentucky, I decided to visit them unexpectedly. I found Genoria Mae lying in bed during school hours. I inquired about her condition, and Helen Mae informed me that she was out of school due to illness.

I briefly left to visit my friends and returned to find a young man sitting on the couch. I asked him who he was, and he responded, "Who are you?'"

So I said, "Okay, I am going to show you who I am," and proceeded to the phone and began to call the police department. He immediately jumped up and ran out of the door. He was on the phone with either Genoria Mae or Lillie Mae, informing them that I was calling the police. They had acquired the same extrinsic motivation as Helen Mae, becoming more loyal to strangers as they were toward me, who had spent tens of thousands of dollars in child support.

Based on my experience with a guy like this, the boyfriend who ran had motives of bad intentions. As far as I was concerned, he might have had intentions to kill Genoria Mae that night, and I was a barrier preventing him from achieving his objective. My experience when it comes to guilt or innocence is that an innocent person would not run, but a guilty person will. This guy ran out the front door as soon as I picked up the phone to call 911. As he began to leave, he started to yell out to Genoria Mae and Lillie Mae that I was calling the police.

Then around 8:00 p.m., Genoria Mae began to dress up in her high heels and fancy dress to accompany this disrespectful boyfriend out—the one who ran when I mentioned calling the police department. I informed Genoria Mae that we could not skip school and date on the same night. She told me that Helen Mae said she could go, but I said she was not leaving.

Then Lillie Mae walked quietly past me. Ten minutes later, the Homewood Police Department arrived and knocked on the door. They announced that they were with the police department, stating that they received a complaint from Lillie Mae regarding Genoria Mae's desire to date the disrespectful man who was waiting for her outside. I informed the police officers that I would not tolerate Genoria Mae's shooting hooky or her missing classes with an excuse of being ill yet going out on the same day even if Helen Mae permitted her.

Then the officers asked if there was a safe place for Genoria Mae to stay for the night (as if I was a stranger), suggesting that she could go back to her grandmother, Kizzy Mae, for a few days. Meanwhile, Lillie Mae informed me that the young man outside was daring me to come out. I told her to tell this disrespectful man who wanted to

A TEEN MARRIAGE CIRCUS

confront me that I would come out and to sit tight. Based on his behavior of wanting to take my life, one can conclude that Genoria Mae was dealing with a man, who reminded me of a Tasmanian devil with his features) with bad intentions, someone who wanted to do bodily harm to her father. At that time, I was a staff sergeant and served as an infantry squad leader / assistant platoon sergeant at Fort Campbell's 101st Airborne / Air Assault Division. The only thing this bad man had to do was to identify himself in a respectful manner, and I would have probably made an exception regarding Genoria Mae's absence from school due to illness and then going out to a party on the same day.

As Lillie Mae quietly walked past me, having called the police earlier, she asked me when I was going out, as if she was encouraging me to endanger my life just like her mother once did. But I told her to tell that disrespectful and irate man she had been communicating with and providing information on what was going on in the apartment to hold on and remain steadfast—I would come out. Interestingly, many years later, when she had a son named John Wayne Robinson, she resorted to punishing him for misconduct, even though I caught her locking him up in the closet. I had to immediately reprimand her and remind her that we had never locked her up in a closet and that I expect to never see this again.

At around 2:00 a.m., I got dressed and adopted the mindset of an infantry soldier confronting the enemies at a time when they were sleeping and not expecting any actions. I prepared myself to proceed down the stairwell and around the corner, using the back of the apartment. Then I proceeded to look for the man, but he was not there. It seemed that he already went out with Genoria Mae since she had gone to Kizzy Mae's apartment, where they had learned not to respect their father as Kizzy Mae and Helen Mae did so often to me.

Unfortunately, because of Genoria's behavior, I had to retrieve the tag from the newly bought Toyota Paseo, a car that I recently purchased. With the aid of the sneaky Lillie Mae, Helen Mae concocted a scheme to trick law enforcement by placing a sheet of paper bearing the handwritten phrase "lost tag" in place of the vehicle's license plate.

Now my objective was to suspend her driving privileges for the weekend until they placed the handwritten note on the car license plate. I returned the vehicle back to the dealership as she had forfeited her right to own a vehicle at the age of sixteen on my watch.

Although she had been raised by the Hatfield, they were not able to buy her a car because they did not have what it took to have one for themselves at that time. They used public transportation as a mode of transportation until I influenced Bobby Joe to be like me and purchased a vehicle, which he did.

Many years later, Genoria Mae informed me that her son needed a vehicle for work, and I suggested that he could get one of my cars since I had three at that time: a 2004 Nissan Altima, the best and most dependable car I have ever owned; a 2014 Nissan Altima that I still drive even up to this day; and a 2003 Custom Dodge. So she came by and retrieved the 2004 Nissan Altima and drove it to her home. I later learned that Genoria Mae gave the car to her other son, who had not received a car from his biological father, the one who raised him. This posed a concern for me because if his son were to be involved in a fatal accident while driving the car, his father would have had every right to be angry with me since the car was derived from my inventory.

Then one day, Genoria Mae called, requesting to withdraw one hundred dollars from our joint savings account to purchase tires for the 2004 Nissan Altima, which I thought was ridiculous because purchasing used tires for a hundred dollars would compromise the safety of the vehicle and put its occupants at risk. In fact, I always purchased tires for this car at $200 each, and they were new tires and not used tires for $100 per set of four. So I instructed her to come and retrieve my 2014 Nissan Altima to meet her mandatory schedule, which involved working and providing transportation for her children since her husband decided to divorce after experiencing the traits shared by Genoria Mae, Kizzy Mae, and Helen Mae, and moved on with his life.

After about eighteen months, Genoria Mae's uncle Billy Joe informed me that she bought a BMW by trading in my favorite car, the 2004 Nissan Altima. I then requested that she return my 2014

Altima, but she informed me that she still needed the car for a few months, and I granted her request. When I inquired about why she traded in my favorite car, which she had never driven or ridden since we had not spoken in years, she said that it had begun to give her a lot of trouble. I then responded, "The reason why the car was giving you a lot of problems is because you were not familiar with the car." This was evident when she returned my 2014 Nissan Altima, and the first thing I noticed was the seat belt light remained illuminated on the passenger side. The cause of this issue was a damaged sensor, likely due to someone placing heavy objects on the seat while operating the vehicle or driving without wearing a seat belt.

Additionally, there was a busted tire rim that needed to be replaced and a missing front electrical cover that could cause a major electrical issue. In other words, it was just a matter of time before this vehicle began to cause major problems as well. Furthermore, the battery required servicing, and I was surprised that it was still able to start the vehicle because of the excessive corrosion buildup around its poles.

Interestingly, because of our strange relationship, Genoria Mae received her driver's license through her high school driver education program, which taught her how to operate a vehicle using an automatic transmission only and subsequently had her baby son to follow the same path that he did obtain his driver's license from the school driver education program.

On the contrary, Lillie Mae came to me for her driving education and training. I took the opportunity to teach her how to operate both vehicles with automatic and standard transmissions, giving her an edge over her sister who only operates a vehicle with an automatic transmission, like the average person today. Even to this day, Genoria Mae only drives an automatic transmission vehicle because of her previous ideology that made her think that she will never be placed in a situation that would require her to operate a vehicle with a manual transmission, something that all Robinsons—except her—can operate.

Being raised by Kizzy Mae, Helen Mae created a flat foot phenomenon with both daughters, allowing them to go barefoot during a time when their foot bones were still forming, which caused them to have flat feet. This pattern was passed down to Helen Mae, who mimicked this behavior that caused some grandchildren to have flat feet. In fact, I was told that one of the grandsons had foot issues because of this phenomenon, creating an issue later that prevented him from joining the armed forces.

Helen Mae had no clue about raising boys or girls. I noticed this when I was visiting her while she was training one of the boys to urinate in a cup before coming downstairs. Instead of going to the restroom, the boy would pass by it and looked for her to give him the cup to urinate. So what I did was when this grandson woke up and before he could go downstairs to find her and the cup, I would direct him to the restroom, letting him know that the appropriate place to urinate was the bathroom since it was next to his bedroom and advising him not look for Grandmother Helen Mae and her cup.

Now when he went downstairs, Helen Mae had noticed something had changed and informed me that I needed to return home, which I did several days later. During those several days, I was able to help another grandson avoid being tormented as Helen Mae would curse him out every day because of him wetting the bed. So one morning, while Helen Mae was downstairs cooking (she could only cook one item at a time) and her grandson Frank Wayne woke up, I immediately assisted him by giving him a set of dry underwear to change into and taught him how to place the wet clothes into the laundry. This was my way to ensure that Helen Mae stopped tormenting him as she did in our relationship, treating him as if he was an adult.

Another weird incident was when she adopted this boy named Christopher, who used to take showers with her under her guidance despite being around ten or eleven years old. One evening, as I entered the bathroom where they were showering, the first thing he did was to close the curtain so I could not see Helen Mae, as if they were lovers, which I found appalling.

This behavior between Helen Mae and Christopher did not stop there. Some nights, when I would spend the night, they would sleep on the same bed while I had to sleep on the floor next to them, pondering whether I was dreaming or experiencing an allusion. During this time, children were excited about this new toy called the Lego, a puzzle containing a group of building blocks where they could construct various creations, such as houses, vehicles, etc. I overheard Helen Mae instructing him not to share it with the other boys, which was something that contradicted the way I was raised as we were trained to share with each other. Not only were my parents adamant about the philosophy of sharing but there was a similar vision at the A. G. Gaston Boys' Club, an organization I participated in during my early childhood.

Now the weirdness continued as Helen Mae—with no experience with proper children development because she did not take the time to learn with me as her supporter, both financially and morally, as she gave our daughter to her mother, Kizzy Mae—now faced with raising children and grandchildren.

So this issue concerned Lillie Mae's daughter Mae Mae, whose nickname was "Meme." One day, I visited without warning, which was the best way to visit a sneaky and disloyal person like Helen Mae. I noticed that Lillie Mae's three children (one boy named Robinson because she was not married at the time of his birth, and two other children born within marriage, whose father made the right decision to divorce her later because he realized that Lillie Mae, his wife, was a replica of Kizzy Mae and Helen Mae) and Genoria Mae's son (last name Robinson, born out of wedlock) were all sitting on the couch, watching a television program. The concerning part was that Helen Mae thought it was okay for the boys to be dressed while the girl was naked as she was nude and unaware of her appearance because her age was around three to four at the time.

As I entered the living room and noticed this behavior, I was appalled. I took Meme from between the boys, who were sitting while she was standing, and gave her to Helen Mae. I ordered her to take her upstairs and dress her as it should have been done from the beginning.

Interestingly, this led to a phenomenon that confused the grandchildren as I had to reside with them in public housing for about a month because Helen Mae had seriously injured her ankle during a fall from leaving her mother's apartment after a serious argument with her. Kizzy Mae made Helen Mae so angry that she missed a step and fell. Now I was tasked to prepare and take them to school. One morning, as I prepared their breakfast, I noticed that the two boys, one her brother and the other her first cousin, were pushing each other and arguing over who was going to sit next to Meme when Helen Mae yelled, "Yawl knock it off and eat your breakfast."

Moreover, Helen Mae would always mock my mother because she wore dentures, and now her teeth were in such bad shape that she talked with her mouth closed or her hand held up, blocking the view of her teeth. I noticed this just recently when she visited and wanted to rekindle our relationship for the third time. This time I said, "No way!"

I said no because I was reminded of a story about a leopard never changing its spots, which allowed me to comprehend that Helen Mae was a doomed cause from day one when Kizzy Mae arranged our marriage. Giving a third opportunity would be a waste of time. Also, there may be signs of insanity in doing the same thing repeatedly and expecting different results—on my part, giving Helen Mae a third chance, knowing that she has been married at least four times that I know about that failed.

Nonetheless, I decided to move on with my education endeavor and career as Helen Mae continued with hers, occasionally taunting me about receiving child support, mocking the justice system, and informing me that she was going to seek more child support, although I was giving her cash on the side for our daughter, including Lillie Mae.

In fact, she called and informed me that she was going to file another petition with the court system to obtain more money. So I contacted Bruce, my attorney, and told him about her comments. He informed me that she had received thousands of dollars over the court-ordered child-support obligations, and he would file a counter claim, seeking to have the money returned if she petitioned the court again. When I called Helen Mae and warned her about the overpayment and the counter claim, that was the last time she mentioned it. On the contrary, she then began to brag about receiving a child-support raise without even asking for it like more cases required to get an increase.

When it came to income tax filing, she would allow other men to use Genoria Mae's and Lillie Mae's social security numbers to claim them, knowing that they were not eligible to do so. They would then split the childcare credit or earned income. I really did not feel responsible for informing the internal revenue service (IRS) to allow Helen Mae and her coconspirators to claim children that I was paying child support because they should have had a mechanism in place to address this abnormality. In fact, Helen Mae was good at hiding things as was in the case of Kizzy Mae, who said she was pregnant when they knew it was not the case.

There was only one time she allowed me to claim them as my children and let me reside with them until the check arrived, which I never did receive because when the check arrived in her mailbox and behind my back, she forged my signature and cashed the check without my knowledge or authorization. It was something that could have sent her to prison for decades for fraud. So several months after the expected timeline had lapsed, I asked her about my federal income tax check repeatedly, and she continued to deny receiving it while giggling.

So out of concern, I went to the IRS and picked up a form that would have tracked down the check if it had been cashed or stolen and prosecuted any illegible activity concerning the person(s) involved with forging the check and cashing it. After completing the form, pulling up near an outdoor mailbox, and out running errands, I called Helen Mae and informed her that I had completed a form from the IRS that would be used to track down the whereabouts of my income tax check and prosecute anyone who has stolen the check.

My final warning to her was if I placed this mail with this completed form addressed to the IRS into the mailbox, I would not be able to stop it from going to the IRS. She then said, "You know that I have stolen the check and cashed it."

My reply was, "You did not have to steal the check. I would have given it to you and that honesty was the best policy."

Before filing my income tax returns, I wrote down all my bills, including hers to pay in full when the check arrives to enhance our credit rating and become debt-free.

Interestingly, I gave her the list to provide feedback about the bills. She drew a line through all the accounts except purchasing tires for the car. I was not surprised at her behavior as she did not want me to become debt-free because it would have opened other opportunities. After she spent my income tax refund, she began to curse me out and call me various names again and refused to open the door after the check discovery had become known.

She always gave me the impression that she was better than me and that I was a nobody. Although, I always tried to monitor Genoria Mae so she would not have an unwedded child as was common for her uncles, who raised her in their home with Kizzy Mae, my conviction of having children remained steadfast within the framework of the bible or divine intervention.

This explained why I married Helen Mae in November 1975 when I thought that Kizzy Mae and she were being truthful when they announced in January 1975 that she was pregnant. In fact, I have never, to this day, seen or signed either Genoria Mae's or Lillie Mae's birth certificates. I can remember vividly requesting her birth certificate when I returned to the regular army for the second time and was told that they were in the mail. Even when I spoke to Kizzy Mae, she also admitted that the birth certificates were in the mail, which never arrived. I could always hear them in the background giggling when they made these testimonies.

Interestingly, what influenced my return to regular army status was when Helen Mae and Kizzy Mae's advisor decided to take me back through the court system and informed them that I was two months late on child support, which paved the way for a new court hearing. I kept in mind what the judge told me about the last time in Helen Mae and Kizzy Mae's presence that he would send me to prison for child support even if I paid the day before like last time.

I must admit that I was two months late in realizing my mistake. I had given her cash on the side, trying to make an amend with her and prevent Genoria Mae's behavior from turning out like hers and Kizzy Mae's. But at the end of the day, Genoria Mae did in fact turn out to be what I now refer to as little Helen. In fact, one of the reasons she never spoke to me as a girl through adulthood was she did not and would not refer to me as "Dad" and knew that calling me by my first name, just as she did my mother, would have been a form of disrespect. And for the record, I have never referred to my parents by their first name as they were my best friend even though they have passed on now—gone to glory.

After returning home and going back to work, unfortunately, after about a year, I had fallen behind in child support payments for a second time. Helen Mae called me, giggling, informing me that she had gone back to the court system and reported that I was in arrears again. She also informed me to let my mother know that the sheriff's office had issued a warrant for my arrest and was looking for me.

Moreover, before going to court the first time for arrears, my mother and I produced the money by using both of our paychecks and borrowing the money from other family members to assist and pay for child support. On the day of the court hearing, I saw Kizzy Mae and Helen Mae sitting in court, giggling, unaware of the fact that I had paid the arrears and was in good standing.

However, when I came before the judge, he leaned over with the rim of his eyewear hanging halfway down his nose and informed me that the next time I would come before him, paying a day before the court would not negate the routine sentence of one year and a day for fathers who fail to pay child support or fall into arrears. You should have seen the look on Kizzy Mae's and Helen Mae's faces when I was told that I could leave because they were hoping for an arrest so the state could assume child support while I serve my time, which never happened.

Later, Helen Mae informed me that she had made a mistake by informing me about her recent deed with the court system, which allowed me to inform my family of her actions and placed my beloved employer where I was a supervisor of about ten workers and a rising star on notice that I had to leave town because Helen Mae and Kizzy Mae had problems with me and wanted to again derail my future and wanted to send me to prison for children that I am not proud of today.

Although Lillie Mae was not my daughter, I was on her birth certificate and she was born while I was still married to Helen Mae while living at separate locations. She lived with Kizzy Mae and her brothers, who were the male figures in their lives. This explained their shortcomings, such as their ability to change an automobile tire in case of emergencies, their lack of understanding about the importance of having and maintaining good credit, and their disregard for the importance of integrity.

While at work, my beloved mother would call me every time the sheriff's office sent a deputy out to append me for child support, which was particularly important since I knew from old friends' recollection about the county jail and their reputation of doing bodily harm to first-timers and people who did not have a criminal record such as myself.

In fact, Helen Mae would always brag about getting me a criminal record to prevent me from reaching my goals and life achievements. In fact, many years later, when I became Farmer Insurance agency owner, she called the telephone company, telling them that I had gone on vacation and to temporarily disconnect the phone system until further notice.

I was made aware of these actions when the district manager called another agent's office, adjacent to my office, inquiring about my phone disconnections. When I inquired about the service by calling the phone company, I was told that my secretary, though I did not have one at the time, called and requested that the phone company temporarily suspend the service due to vacation. Later, I asked Helen Mae about the misdeed. She giggled and informed me that she placed a woman's scorn on me and that she was not going to allow me to own or be successful in the insurance business.

So I had to tell my family goodbye, but I never let Kizzy Mae and Helen Mae know of my intentions of leaving the town and returning to the regular army, where I could create an allotment and never be late again. Although I had no intentions of returning to regular army status, this allowed me to stay free from the court system

A TEEN MARRIAGE CIRCUS

and ensure that my child-support obligation could be met. In fact, when the allotment started, the arrest warrant was negated through the court system.

Matter of fact, I had to fly to Atlanta, Georgia, because the army did not have an opening until later that year—that was in 1988. After returning to regular army status and resuming child support through an automatic deduction by way of an allotment, I received a call from Helen Mae, acknowledging that she had made a serious mistake in informing me that she had returned to the court system. This revelation prevented my arrest and the fulfillment of her goal to ruin my reputation by having a criminal record. However, this also ensured me that she would succeed in getting me arrested the next time as she feared that I would seek greater endeavors.

Now the first time I was on regular army active status, I could not wait until my term was up, but the second time around was to stay until Genoria Mae and Lillie Mae reached the age of majority. This way I would be rid of my financial obligation to Helen Mae, who was being coached by her mother, Kizzy Mae. Too many times she has told me that her mother was the mastermind behind her ruined marriage with me. She has always said, "If I hadn't listened to my mother, I would be with my husband now."

Regardless of Helen Mae's history of lacking honesty and strong moral principles, as well as name-calling and acting with no respect toward me, I still attempted to work with her because of our daughter Genoria Mae and Charles's daughter, Lillie Mae. In fact, when I entered the army for the second time, I was assigned to a multitask operation (MFO) located in the country of Egypt, monitoring various operations in the surrounding sea. Now because of my education and being a graduate of the University of Alabama, earning a degree in political science and sociology paved the way for me to teach my fellows courses that led to over twenty degrees, thus propelling some of them for the promotions to senior ranks.

As an instructor at Central Texas College, I earned four hundred dollars per student, making a tremendous amount of money that I would send back home to Helen Mae as an extra incentive to raise our children in a manner that would bolster their livelihood and start a home-base business named ABVAN Administration Agency, a family-owned company that I dreamed would become a multi-million-dollar operation designated to pass down the children and grandchildren, in addition to the allotment that satisfied my child-support obligations.

My best friend and fellow soldier, Sergeant Franklin Webster, warned me about sending Helen Mae that tremendous amount of money to start a home-base business without supervision that was not available since I was serving an assignment that placed me out of the United States at the time.

Sergeant Webster predicted, without knowing her, that Helen Mae would abuse the opportunity to move our new company in a positive direction because he felt that she did not have the expertise to handle such a challenge, such as serving as chief executive officer of a company without proper education and expertise that she did not originate nor having any business training or education above a twelve-grade education, which was one of our problems as I later learned.

In hindsight, I realized that Helen Mae was not the right person for me and thought that I could change her behavior because we had a child that was doomed because of deceit and misrepresentation of facts from Kizzy Mae from the beginning.

Although this was my worst experience, I still felt like we could achieve the American dream of starting a new venture, owning a home, and raising a family without having children or grandchildren born out of wedlock. However, as previously discussed, this was not the case for Charles's daughter, Lillie Mae, who has moved on with her life and terminated all communication with me since reaching adulthood.

Interestingly, when Lillie Mae was growing up, she would always pretend that she was remarkably close to me until reaching adulthood. In fact, the last time I saw her was driving down the Fairfield City road that we were both traveling on. And when she looked over and recognized it was me, she then accelerated and sped off, as if she had not seen me. I was amused by her actions but acknowledged that she was a product of Kizzy Mae and Helen Mae's training and upbringing.

However, when it came to our new venture, the ABVAN Administration Agency, Lillie Mae was not patient as she expected overnight success.

Nevertheless, the name ABVAN was derived from my combining both of our names, Abraham and Helen Mae, but using a few letters to create this future business. The only requirement was she had to keep a roster of the business expenditures regarding the extra money that was sent from my time as an instructor from Central College of Texas and follow up on prospects concerning new business that I was procuring while serving oversea, as well as fulling the orders and providing outstanding customer service.

Well, when I returned from Egypt, I visited Helen Mae and found out that her list of expenditures consisted of expenses that were not business-related, such as potato chips, clothes, shoes, vacations, etc. Nonetheless, I continued to show support for acquiring a business venture with a person who had been very disrespectful to me and my family by calling us names and mocking members who wore dentures.

Moreover, the start of ABVAN Administration Agency's day-to-day operations was handled by Helen Mae while I served out my remaining active-duty contract at Fort Campbell. With proximity to the great state of Alabama, I could commute a four-hour journey, visit them, and check on Genoria Mae and our newly formed business.

Our business design was to secure various federal, state, city, and local business contracts, dealing with billing, printing, and providing general administration. Well, I purchased a booklet from a small business administration that focused on women and minority-owned businesses to seek out opportunities for minorities and to bolster our knowledge about ways to enhance our newly formed venture.

Interestingly, one day I made an unannounced visit to Helen Mae's apartment, where I was paying the rent in addition to child support. While Helen was out, I answered a phone call from a gentleman asking for her. I informed him that she was not home at the time and asked if he wanted to leave a message. He replied, "Let Helen Mae know that they were watching me at work, and I could not help her without being terminated."

I informed him that I would give her his message. When she arrived back at the apartment, I briefed her on the phone call and the message that was left and informed her that our business was not going to be built on pilfering or misconduct.

After the briefing, I continued to secure business opportunities from the book I had purchased from the chamber of commerce and a new business, such as producing business cards and flyers that were sent out before I returned to the army base. Interestingly, Lillie Mae's daughter was more involved in the venture than Genoria Mae's, who was still in Kizzy Mae's shell and not speaking to me, unlike her half sister who would accompany me to the post office where we sent out orders for our new clients. Our company policies allowed us to send merchandise, along with the invoice, allowing the customer to send payment within ninety days.

In fact, Lillie Mae would always question me about when the money was going to start to come in. I informed her that it was imperative that we do our part first and that the money and the rewards would come later. And it did after I returned to the army base at Fort Cambell, where I was stationed, according to Helen Mae's report when I spoke to her on the phone about our new venture.

*****

On the night that Lillie Mae called the Homewood Police Department on me about Genoria Mae's shooting hooky and school absence, it came to light that she was planning to go on a date with the male suspect who was very disrespectful toward me and a close friend of Helen Mae. As I informed her about the incident, she took Genoria Mae's disrespectful and dangerous boyfriend's side as she did with all strange men in the past.

After Helen Mae sided with him, I informed her that I was not going to pay their rent and utilities anymore and that she had thirty days to vacate this luxury apartment and return to the government projects as they were called where they were raised since she sided with this stranger who was taking Genoria Mae out that the night in question.

Interestingly, before the incident, Genoria Mae and Lillie Mae were kicked out of school for misconduct as they asked Helen Mae to purchase them a bell that they could ring. So Helen Mae contacted me and informed me that they had been expelled from high school because the bell she had purchased was being used to mock as they would ring the bell at other girls and call them the *B* word every time they saw them during breaktime walking up and down the hallways.

Although I was not surprised since they were raised by Kizzy Mae and Helen Mae, with little to no supervision, this behavior was imminent. It was just a matter of time and opportunity. So I took emergency leave from Fort Cambell to get them reinstated so they would not have to attend an alternate school for children with discipline and behavioral issues as was displayed with my experience with their mother, Helen Mae.

The next day, I informed them to prepare to return to school when Charles's daughter told me that Helen Mae had attempted to reenroll them, but the administrators denied her request. Again, I repeated myself and told them to get ready to return to school, and Lillie Mae said, "Okay, just remember we told you that Helen Mae's request was denied." Lillie Mae spoke on behalf of Genoria Mae.

So when we reported to the school administrator's office, we waited for the principal to arrive. He came in about thirty minutes after school had started and noticed that I was wearing my dress greens, a complete military uniform with all ribbons and badges attached, which was impressive as he thanked me for my service. Before our conversation, I asked Genoria Mae and Lillie Mae to step outside so I could have a head-to-head conference with their principal about their misconduct. I informed him that I do not condone misconduct and will not tolerate children raised by the Hatfield family to misrepresent the Robinson family. It was important to ask them to step outside during our meeting, considering the training they received from Kizzy Mae and Helen Mae over the years.

I pleaded to him to give them another chance to complete their high school education and swore that if they'd give the school or the administrator any more problems, I would personally remove them from their institutions and send them to an alternative school for girls with behavioral problems. The principal concurred. But I needed to convey this conversation to them so they would be aware of any consequence that would be derived if they'd violate our agreement.

I opened the principal's door and invited them back into the conference room. The principal explained to them, "Your daddy will explain what will happen next." I then informed them that they had been reinstated and that if the school, principal, or administrator had any more problems with them, I would personally withdraw them and enroll them in an alternative school for girls with behavior issues. The principal wrote a note for them to carry to their instructors, admitting them into class to resume their studies, which subsequently led to their graduation from one of the most prominent schools in the state of Alabama.

However, that afternoon, after I stopped over at Kizzy Mae's home where Helen Mae, Genoria Mae, and Lillie Mae were present. Kizzy Mae began to yell at me, calling me various slave names and informing me that I had sided with the white principal and not with my own children who displayed misconduct that they learned from being raised by the Hatfield family.

Instead of bragging about me doing what it took to get them back into school for misconduct, I just shook my head and laughed because I knew by then that she was a deceitful lady who lied about her daughter's pregnancy to rid herself of a rebellious daughter who displayed unbelievable behavior.

Interestingly, it was later revealed that the school suspension debacle was done by Lillie Mae, who turned out to be the mastermind behind it. We later found out that she had gotten pregnant while attending high school and was jealous of the other girls who made better choices than she did.

In fact, she and Helen Mae had concealed this pregnancy from me until that summer when Lillie Mae decided to take a summer job for students and complained about the free food that was avail-

A TEEN MARRIAGE CIRCUS

able. This was an example of the arrogant behavior learned from the Hatfield.

When this revelation was brought to my attention, I returned home from Fort Campbell to take Lillie Mae and shop for groceries at Walmart, the largest supermarket in town, and allowed her to purchase any food of her choice to negate her negative attitude about her new summer job not providing food that would prevent her from working and gaining a positive experience from earning money the appropriate way.

I was supposed to spend the night to personally prepare her lunch for the next day, but then she and Helen Mae had a private meeting. Helen informed me that she advised Lillie Mae to better go and let me know that she had been terminated from that job and was unable to perform her duties that required her participation in extreme heat because of pregnancy.

Helen Mae informed me that she told Lillie Mae that I got up in the morning to prepare her lunch and expected to take her to her new job and finding out that she no longer worked there would highly upset me. She suggested going in there and letting me know now.

Well, that night, before bedtime, she came in and spoke to me, letting me know that she had quit the job and I did not need to prepare her lunch the next day, and exited the room without saying anything else. Although I was extremely disappointed with her actions, I knew from experience since Kizzy Mae and Helen Mae were also dishonest about the January 1975's announcement date of her daughter's pregnancy. Now with Genoria Mae and Lillie Mae being raised and taught to be dishonest as the norm, it was not her fault.

In fact, the only time Helen Mae told the truth was when she bragged about allowing any man except me to have an intimacy relationship with her. I can still remember her exact words that day: "You're just mad because everyone can get it except you, and we are married," which I mentioned earlier in this manuscript. One point to note is that I have never seen either of Genoria Mae's or Lillie Mae's bellies protruding to indicate that they were pregnant, but I saw their fatherless babies after the fact.

Although Genoria Mae did not have a baby during her high school years, it did not take long for her to get pregnant once she left for college. Interestingly, if you thought Lillie Mae was sneaky about her ordeal, Genoria Mae kept her pregnancy secret until her due date, according to Helen Mae. I was always kept blinded about her ordeal even to this day as I have never seen her pregnant. She now have three children, a testament of Kizzy Mae and Helen Mae creating an environment where we do not speak even to this day.

Yes, I was disappointed because they were producing children without being married and giving them the Robinson's last name when the children's last name should have been after their fathers, whom I have never met even to this day. In addition, I had to provide financial support for their stability and growth because their fathers had vanished with known interactions that did not exist.

Now this unwedded childbirth phenomenon was not surprising because their uncle, who assisted in raising them, had a lot of children from different women and was also not married. So one could conclude from a father's perspective that this behavior was imminent because of a lack of supervisor and being raised in an environment where Kizzy Mae and Helen Mae and the uncles had a problem with candor.

Moreover, after getting them back in school, now it was time to discipline Helen Mae for siding with Genoria Mae for missing school and for going out with a stranger who arrived that night to take her on a date. I had warned Helen Mae that she had thirty days to vacate the luxury apartment, which she ignored and continued to reside there. So what I did was I terminated the rent by not paying it and stopping her army allotment for one month, knowing that this would be devastating and would pave the way for eviction from this apartment, which it did. She had to return to public housing where she was raised along with Genoria Mae and Lillie Mae, a place that they were familiar with from birth.

In fact, their behavior reminded me of something I heard as a child from a lady everyone called Miss Helen. She said, "You can take a person out of the country, but you cannot take the country out of the person."

A TEEN MARRIAGE CIRCUS

Now when I correlate their behavior pattern, including Helen Mae, Genoria Mae, Lillie Mae, and their uncle, I was reminded that you can take them out of public housing, but you cannot take public housing out of them, which explained what I have experienced with this entire Hatfield family.

After the school suspension incident, I returned to Fort Campbell and continue with my military assignment until one day out of nowhere, I decided to return to the apartment to ensure Helen Mae had vacated. When I looked out of the window, I noticed a huge man getting out of a car. The man appeared to be a gangster as I looked on. He passed over twenty-five units until he reached Helen Mae's apartment. When he knocked on the door and requested to use the phone, I informed him that he needed to go to the nearest gas station, which was only two city blocks away to use the public phone. I later learned this was a newly formed relationship that Helen Mae had established with him, and when I answered the door, he used the phone as a distraction because he did not expect me to be present at the time.

Moreover, when she finally vacated the apartment and returned to public housing, I stopped by, but Helen Mae refused to let me in to her new apartment, even though she had a habit of leaving her door open for anyone to enter at their discretion. In fact, when I transitioned from regular army to part-time army reservist and began a new career in the insurance business, this gave me the opportunity to move around the city to seek prospects and serve old clients.

With this achievement, I became the district leader in sales and collections at United Insurance under the management of District Manager Tannehill. He requested that I brief the other agents on the techniques that I was using to achieve such success. In regard to collections, I informed the other agents that I would provide free postage to new clients as an incentive to mail their payments on time.

During the sales closing process, I would explain to the prospects that when they receive my invoice with prepaid postage, it doesn't mean that the bill is due then. Instead, it serves as a reminder to send their payment as soon as possible. This simple technique proved to be beneficial as it gave my clients the opportunity to prioritize their monthly bills and make payments according to their financial status.

As a result of my efficiency, I received an opportunity to transfer to a corporate office located on Wacker Drive in Chicago, Illinois, where you will find many skyscrapers. However, one of the requirements was to send a resume and cover letter. So I showed the announcement to Helen Mae and asked her to prepare a resume, send it, and cooperate, and she promised to do so. At this time, we had started a new venture called ABVAN Administration Agency, where she had possession of all the office equipment that I had purchased before leaving Fort Campbell.

So I stopped by one afternoon and decided to wait on the resume so I could forward it to the corporate. Helen Mae took about five hours to go through all her cluttered paperwork, including past due invoices while I waited for the resume. When she completed her personal task, something that should not have existed from the beginning, she then turned on the computer, selected a file, and printed an obsolete resume. Before I could question her about it, she jumped up and proceeded to walk upstairs without even acknowledging that I was talking to her.

So I left with an obsolete resume and called her later about creating an up-to-date resume. She then said, "No problem. I will update it and send it to corporate for you." Several days later, I called her about the updated resume, and she said, "Okay, I took care of it." I asked her about the cover letter, and she said, "I sent it too." I asked her who signed the cover letter, and she then began to curse me out, calling me various names, and hung the phone up in my face. I later called the corporation, and they informed me that they had not received it, and the position was now filled.

As a result, my good fortune continued when I received a call from Farmer Insurance, inviting me for an interview. I was informed that if I met certain benchmarks, I could become an agency owner. Well, after informing Helen Mae about this opportunity, she called the telephone company one day, without my consent, and informed them that she was my secretary and requested the phone to be temporarily cut off because I was going on vacation.

A TEEN MARRIAGE CIRCUS

This misdeed was brought to light when my new district manager called and complained about my phone being disconnected. I told him that I would contact the phone to inquire about the phone service. That was when I found out about Helen Mae's misdeed. I ordered the phone company to reinstate services immediately, which they did. Nonetheless, the service had been off for about two weeks, and I had no clue it was off since I was in the field, working door-to-door and in person, prospecting. When I confronted Helen Mae about this misdeed, she replied that this was an example of a "woman's scorn"—something that she would repeat many times thereof.

Interestingly, one day I had to ask her to drop me off at the Farmer Insurance, and this man who she referred to as Cornbread—someone who grew up in the same public housing that she did and someone who communicated with me every day for about ten to twenty minutes—was the janitor of the office building.

As I walked past him and entered the men's restroom, he followed me inside and asked me a weird question that was overly concerning that I later told Helen Mae, and she told me to wait until I see him again. The question Cornbread asked me was, "Is Helen Mae still dropping her drawers?" I was appalled by this question, but I informed him about our daughter, and from that point on, he never spoke to me again.

While I was out prospecting, going door-to-door, I stumbled upon Cornbread's house. He was not home at the time, but his wife invited me inside to discuss their homeowner insurance needs. She called Cornbread to let him know that an insurance agent was there, and he authorized her to go ahead and purchase a new homeowner policy since they were uninsured.

As I began the sales and application process, Cornbread arrived and was startled to see me and informed his wife that he did not want the insurance and told me to leave immediately. I knew once I saw Cornbread that this sale was dead on arrival because of his comments about Helen Mae and their previous relation.

*****

Moreover, Lillie Mae asked me to employ her as an office manager so she could gain experience in the corporate world to establish a platform for greater endeavors and enhance her resume. Although I was concerned about her behavior and her upbringing since she was raised by Kizzy Mae and Helen Mae, who were the worst people I have ever encountered, I still employed her and assigned her the title of office manager.

So I sent her to the district office for office manager training, and the first thing the district office complained about was her attire and morale. Her starting pay was five hundred dollars per week, with the office paying her taxes, including her social security and Medicare.

Now at the end of her first week, after receiving five hundred dollars on Friday, she came in on the following Monday before I could get started. She began to ask for more money, and I told her that I did not have time to discuss money as payday was scheduled for Friday. She began to mumble, and I told her she could go home because I had work to complete because of the required benchmarks set forth by corporate that must be met.

She then left and decided to join the army. During the base training, she informed me that the female drill sergeant was discriminating against her by not counting her push-up exercise correctly and showing favoritism toward the other women.

To stay in the army, Lillie Mae concocted a story that allowed her to take an emergency leave as a final measure to prevent an early discharge and showed that she was unfit to serve because she had issues regarding her weakness as the sets of training were related to physical activities—something that contrasted my results as an infantry squad leader and the one who took part in many physical activities and special operations.

*****

When she returned home, I was serving the army reserve at the time and asked her to perform some push-ups and discovered that she was unable to do one push-up correctly. She giggled when I asked her to start, and I was unable to give her even one push-up.

Although she was able to do several sit-ups correctly but also had issues with finishing the mandatory two-mile run, I was able to figure out her weakness and devised a plan of action that required her to allow me to show her some techniques, such as going out to my alma mater, Lawson State Community College, every morning, using their track field to run with her, showing the same technique I would use in my own running challenge. Whenever she felt exhausted, I would have her turn and run backward to change the dynamic of the wind so she could not breathe it head-on, and then we would run up and down the hill off the track, leaving for the school in a jungle-like environment.

Then once we finished the run, we then went ahead to the pull-up bars and started to go up and down as I aided her by holding her legs at the ankle for support. I would push her up as she began to struggle to go up. Once we finished this exercise, we went back to Helen Mae's apartment to use her stairwell to continue to improve her cardiovascular system and build her upper body and lower body muscle group, which was paramount to successfully passing the army's minimum mandatory physical fitness test.

After that, we began the push-up exercises while I would stand over her with my hands tethered to the back of her sweatshirt, using a technique that would push her down as she resisted while pulling her up when she began to struggle coming up. I would then use an old football exercise to strengthen her abdominal muscles by standing in front near her head while she was on her back. With her legs up together in a ninety-degree position, I would throw her legs down at three different angles while recommending that she resist building her stomach muscles.

We would always stretch before and after each exercise regimen to ensure that she understood the importance of loosening up before exercising to prevent injury and maximize her potential to successfully pass the physical fitness test.

Interestingly, during the two furloughs, and to her credit, she would self-test herself and give me a daily update on her progress. It was extraordinary as she increased her push-up, sit-up, and two-mile running abilities to meet the physical fitness test before returning to her base at Fort Jackson, South Carolina. Now when she returned and passed the test, she informed me that her drill sergeants were impressed with her receiving the highest score and wanted to know who helped in her transformation.

She replied, "My dad." She was told, according to her briefing that I need to become a drill sergeant to help other female soldiers who had issues in passing the army's standard physical fitness test. Yes, I was flattered to hear that I had created a positive experience for Lillie Mae, showing her that it was not discrimination, but rather it was her not being ready for the challenge.

And as far as credit for my participation, I would have to quote from Dr. Martin Luther King, someone that I remember in 1968 when I was eleven years old on the night he was assassinated in Memphis, Tennessee. He once said, "If I can help someone as I pass along, if I can cheer somebody with a word or song, if I can show somebody he's traveling wrong, then my living will not be in vain."

Ironically, this was not the first time that Lillie Mae, who was raised by Kizzy Mae, Helen Mae, and her uncles who claimed someone was discriminating against her as was the case in high school, took part in the Air Force's ROTC program. At this time, I was on active duty at Fort Campbell, serving as a squad leader and aid platoon sergeant. When I came home for a weekend visit, I noticed that she was complaining about the school's ROTC instructors who were showing favoritism toward the white male students in terms of their outstanding uniform appearance and badge placement.

After listening to her complaints and noticing that her uniform was wrinkled and had spots on it, I realized that it did not meet the military standards. I couldn't help but think that if she were in my squad, she would have had valid reasons to complain about me as well. So I recommended Lillie Mae to begin sending her uniforms to a professional cleaner at my expense, and I retrieved an official display to show how ribbons and badges are worn, then I took her professionally cleaned uniform and, using the display, showed her how to place ribbons and badges, according to the Air Force and military standards. I let her know my expectation was the same as her instructors.

During the next ROTC class, she won best dress and was surprised that discrimination was not the resolution for enhancing her performance, and in fact, the instructors were looking for future officers to show excellency, which started with their attire. Giving her an unsatisfactory grade for her appearance was a way to improvement.

Moreover, once Lillie Mae had completed her army's physical fitness test, she was sent to the next level, which was advanced individual training (AIT), at the same military installation. After about three months in advance training, Helen Mae informed me that Lillie Mae reported a sexual assault, pressing charges against another male soldier from the navy that she had been raped. The soldier faced a court-martial, but fortunately, the charges against him were dropped when other female soldiers came forward and informed the chain of command that Lillie Mae had told them that she was angry that the male soldier would not have a relationship with her and this was her way to get even with him.

Let me digress here about Lillie Mae's false accusation and comment on something that her mother, Helen Mae, did to me while I was serving in the Army reserves. One day, she called me and requested that I take her to the hotel so we could make up and be physically intimate. As soon as she took off her clothes while I was still dressed, she began to curse me out and call me names and attempt to leave the hotel room without any clothes on. I restrained her because it became apparent for her motive to get me in serious trouble since all else had failed. She had tunnel vision that day as her only focus was to get out of the front door without any clothes on. So I had to use psychological tactics on her to convince her to put her clothes back on, and after fifteen minutes or so of ranting, she complied. I took her home, and she never mentioned that ordeal to anyone. But from that day on, when she mentioned sex, I recommended her to call someone else because I was done with her. So when Lillie Mae's sexual assault ordeal came up, I thought about Helen Mae.

Once this revelation was exposed, Lillie Mae was discharged from the army for misconduct and was sent home in the best interest of the military. Interestingly, when she had reported the sexual assault, Helen Mae told me that she asked Lillie Mae why she did not report the incident to me. She had no answer. In fact, the reason she did not report the incident to me was that she knew where I stood when it came to integrity and candor.

Let's go back to when Lillie Mae was in middle school, a time when Kizzy Mae and Helen Mae were complaining about her homework and grades, not realizing that they had created this dilemma. I began to help her with her homework, which was something that they did not have time for. One evening, after helping her with an assignment, I entered the door of the public housing where she was residing, Kizzy Mae and Helen Mae began to yell and giggle at me saying, "You helped her, but she still failed the test and earned an *F*." So I instructed Lillie Mae to meet me in the living room to review her assignment that I helped her with.

As I began reviewing the homework, I noticed that the answer we had the day before had been changed. I could see the erased answers that had been substituted. I asked Lillie Mae who changed these answers, and she leaned over and whispered to me saying that she had earned an *A* but was afraid to let Kizzy Mae and Helen Mae know out of fear that she would be disciplined. She asked me not to say anything to them about her changing her answers to receive an *F*.

While we were on this subject matter, during my service stationed in Germany, Helen Mae contacted me regarding a science project that the children were struggling with. A project about static electricity was assigned to Genoria Mae while a topic about understanding the phenomena of biodegradable was assigned to Lillie Mae. Now I personally did both projects and mailed them to them and later learned that Genoria Mae earned an *A* while Lillie Mae had earned an *F*.

So when I asked Lillie Mae about the failing grade, my first question was, "Do you like your teacher?" and her response was, "I hate my teacher." I then recommended that if she hated her teacher, then the feeling was mutual. But the teacher had the upper hand, and her feeling toward her teacher could have affected her grade.

A TEEN MARRIAGE CIRCUS

During my own academic journey, while pursuing my doctorate degree in performance psychology at Ashford University and Grand Canyon University, I was a college instructor at Texas Central College and had a disrespectful student. He received the grade he earned instead of using a scaling system that could have pushed him over the top to a passing grade. Moreover, Lillie Mae could have changed her grade as she did in middle school. In addition, She came to me, complaining about her teammates on the girls' basketball team. She said that no one would toss her the ball when she was able to score, but instead, they would wait until she turned her head away from the ball, and let someone then tossed her the ball, which hit her in the back or in her face when she turned to receive it.

In reference to Genoria Mae, unlike her sister, she did not have a baby in high school. However, it did not take long for her to have a baby once she left home and went to college. Unfortunately, the fathers of her children did not take part in their lives, both financially and morally.

In fact, I have never seen either of these men until Facebook came into focus, and Lillie Mae's son became grown and his father reached out to me, along with other family members, bragging about their relationship. On Facebook, I asked all these family members, including his father, "Where were you all when I had to pay hundreds of thousands of dollars to raise your son?"

He said on Facebook that it was not his fault because Lillie Mae was out of control and would not allow him to take part in his son's life. The first things that came to my mind were Kizzy Mae and Helen Mae since they would not allow me to be with my children but needed child support to help with their own financial deficiencies.

Moreover, while attending high school, I bought Lillie Mae a car of her choice, which was a Honda Accord. Then on the first day of owning this vehicle, she allowed her son to play with the gear shift while driving and, in some kind of way, managed to move the stick shift, thus putting the car into reverse while going forward. This action at once caused the vehicle to stop in the middle of the road while idling.

When I arrived onsite and inquired about what happened, Lillie Mae simply said, "Nothing, it just happened by itself. We were just driving, and it just stopped." I had the car returned to the dealership via wrecker service where the mechanics confirmed my suspicion that someone had forced the gear out of place. As I arrived on site, I noticed that Lillie Mae's son was sitting in the front seat with the gear shift in reverse instead of the drive position. I did not say anything because I knew who raised her, and now the domino theory was in effect. The domino theory was the belief during the Vietnam War that if we could topple one Southeast Asian country, the rest would fall.

One day, while meeting Genoria Mae at Helen Mae's public housing, she made a statement to me on the stairwell. One day when I was counseling her about her behavior, she said, "Look, Dad, when you speak to me, you need to say something that you know I want to hear. If not, I will start remembering things that never happened." This serves as another example of the domino theory that had been passed down to the grandchildren.

As I was leaving Helen Mae's apartment, Lillie Mae's son John Wayne begged me to take him home because he wanted to spend the night.

John Wayne requested that we stop by the store first, and I did. I allowed him to purchase anything he wanted, and when we got within one city block of my mother's home, where I was living, he then turned to me and said, "You can turn around now and take me back home," which I did.

Several weeks later, he and I stopped by my mother's home. My mother gave John some cookies, and he took the cookies from my mother's hand and threw them into the trash can, which is something I have always remembered to this day. Kizzy Mae raised this boy and taught him to hate the Robinsons as he did even to this day.

Now when John reached the age of majority, under the supervision of Kizzy Mae and Lillie Mae, he decided to sell marijuana. Interestingly, during his first day of operation, he was detained and arrested for distribution of a controlled substance. His bail was set at

$1500 of which I paid half and made Kizzy Mae and Lillie Mae pay the balance since they had raised him from birth.

Then I went to post his bond at the county jail, and the first thing he asked for was a hamburger and a milkshake to which I obliged. During our drive home, I asked him what type of drug dealer he was to get arrested on the first day of business. His response was he needed money, so I proposed that he focus on school and I would pay him $200 per week.

The following week, on Friday, I paid him the agreed-upon amount of $200. However, the next day, I was tasked to take him to Saturday school, and as he began to exit the car door, he asked for five dollars. I responded, "You just got paid yesterday."

His response was, "I gave the money to my mother."

"I will always keep some of my pay even if it's only five dollars," I replied as I gave him five dollars as requested and went on my way.

Then the next day, his mother called and said that he had been arrested again. I told them that I was not going to bond him out because he thought this matter of incarceration was a joke and that he needed to learn that I was not going to tolerate this type of behavior.

Nonetheless, one day I stopped by Helen Mae's apartment, and an angry man just walked in without knocking, which was not necessary since it was a customary practice to leave the door ajar. This habit of hers of leaving doors open made her feel comfortable, a behavior she learned from Kizzy Mae during her time living in one of the most dangerous neighborhoods in America.

The man came in and cursed me out, calling me various names, as I was appalled because I had never seen him before. I told him that I did not know him and became silent because I was in fear for my life, which, again, reminded me of what Helen Mae told me about no dying and that some man would take my life.

After the unknown angry man and Helen Mae had spoken in private, she returned. I then asked her what his problem was, but she just walked by and said nothing about the incident. Again, visiting Helen Mae in public housing had begun to put me at risk of losing my life. I had to beg her not to open the door one night when a man was challenging me to come outside while banging on the door.

After moving on and residing with my supportive family, I later learned that Helen Mae had married again a man named Fred, a person her brother referred to as a "grave digger." He and Helen Mae called me, with her name appearing on the caller ID. She then handed the phone to Fred, whom I never met. He began to curse me out and threatened to come to my family's home if I did not answer his question about whether I had met with his wife, Helen Mae, while he was at work the day he ordered her to call me, which gave me the impression that it was her calling for herself instead of calling for him.

Although I knew from experience that Helen Mae was capable of cheating on her husband as she did with me while working in Pascagoula, Mississippi, in fear, I politely answered his question so he would not visit my home and bring harm to my family. In fact, I ran into them at the grocery store, a place I had never visited before. He approached me and began informing me that Helen Mae was his wife, now bearing the surname Dawson.

So as a strategic move and to mitigate his concerns about Helen Mae, I jokingly stated to him, "As it relates to his wife, Helen Mae, I just want to thank you," a comment that Helen Mae later called, informing me to never say anything like that again because every time they get into a fight, he would bring it up in a derogatory manner.

Interestingly, the business that I started with Helen Mae called ABVAN began to evolve into a tax preparation service that would provide rapid processing and the option to receive a check within forty-eight hours, or about two days, through a direct loan association with a bank that would receive a portion of the return to process the advance loan. I allowed them to prepare my tax returns until one day, Fred and Helen Mae fought, and he informed me that he decided to hold my check to show that he oversaw the company I started. I replied, "No problem." But I later informed Lillie Mae that this would be my last time during business with Fred's tax agency. In fact, after pondering the acronym ABVAN, Fred ordered Helen Mae to change the name from ABVAN to Tax Solutions.

I was now an agency owner, selling multiline insurance products, covering homes, automobiles, renters, life, and commercial insurance. When Helen Mae came by the midfield office, requesting a policy for her and Fred's tax service that covered the various types of personal losses, I did comply and regretted it later.

At the end of the tax season, just before vacating the building, Helen Mae and Fred filed a burglary claim, which my agency ended up paying the expenses. After the claim was paid, I placed Helen Mae and Fred's tax service on the "do not renew" list. When she called about a new policy, I informed her that they were substantially risky and needed to purchase from another carrier.

Several weeks later, Helen Mae called me regarding her homeowner insurance and wanted to purchase one from my agency since she was uninsured. Now, against my best judgment and with reluctance, I went out to inspect their home while Fred was at work and noticed during the inspection of the detached garage that they had stored items that appeared they claimed earlier were stolen during their recent burglary. Once I noticed these items, I thought about the ole saying, "Fool me once, shame on you. Fool me twice, shame on me." So I did not say anything about my discovery because it appeared odd with the equipment, but there were doubts, so I decided to place her on my permanent "do not insure" list.

One thing that bothered me was when my mother passed away, the only way the Hatfield family found out about her illness was when her brother Billy Joe would visit my mother's home behind my back, as if we had a good relationship, and then go back and brief his mother, Kizzy Mae, and Helen Mae of her condition. They had never visited each other or even had any respect to attend her funeral as they knew they would not be welcomed.

One day, I went to the funeral home, and surprisingly, I saw Kizzy Mae, Helen Mae, and Fred, mocking my mother's death as I could not even speak to them. I had never seen them happier that day. I was appalled that they were viewing my mother because Helen Mae would always mock my mother's appearance due to her denture.

On the other hand, when Kizzy Mae became ill, I did not visit or even inquire about her condition as I could easily remember all the deceitfulness she had bought into my life, including her pointing that 22-caliber pistol at me as previously mentioned earlier.

In fact, before her demise, she had been hospitalized for surgery, and Lillie Mae begged me to visit her because she wanted to see me. But I reluctantly said no to her because meeting this lady and the Hatfield family was a nightmare that created a strained relationship that persists to this day. We do not speak to each other, including Helen Mae, Genoria Mae, Lillie Mae, and their children.

Something else that rattled me was whenever I would talk to Helen Mae on the phone, which was rare. I could hear a lot of background noises, giggling, and loud talking. Even though our conversation was about me explaining my dissatisfaction with her behavior and how I hated ever meeting her, she would sarcastically say before hanging the phone up my face, "I love you too," which was something I have never said to her even to this day.

*****

Moreover, another issue rose when we moved into a second luxury apartment. On our first night, she informed me that her back was hurting, so she had to go to the store to buy some back pain cream called Bengay, which creates a hot stinging feeling as the direction recommended using a very thin and small amount of cream on the affected area. Once, I used this cream and massaged it onto the affected area, including the rhomboid and the latissimi dorsi muscle, and the pain immediately dissipated.

Then several weeks later, I asked Helen Mae to massage my back using the same cream. Guess what she did? She took the tube and squeezed the entire contents, emptying the tube, and took the edge of it to spread onto my back while giggling. I had to run to the shower and wash it off my back. I referred to this as the last back rub as I never asked her again to do so.

Additionally, while living in Pascagoula, Mississippi, I asked Helen Mae to prepare my lunch one day. She said, "God gave you a hand," which was something that I never forgot, not to mention that she giggled and continued to watch the television.

Regarding the Christmas debacle and the strained relationship between me, Kizzy Mae, Helen Mae, and the Hatfield family,

I have never spent a single holiday with them. However, one year, I received a call from Helen Mae, informing me that they wanted to surprise Kizzy Mae's grandchildren Genoria Mae and Lillie Mae for Christmas by purchasing thousands of dollars worth of toys, including clothes and hiding them at my mother's home and asked me to deliver them after midnight while they were asleep for Christmas morning.

Helen Mae and I agreed to surprise Kizzy Mae's grandchildren, as well as pay for the credit charges later since they had financial issues that prevented them from paying cash. At around 5:00 p.m. on Christmas Eve, Helen Mae, Genoria Mae, and Lillie Mae showed up to retrieve the Christmas items. When I asked Helen Mae about the surprise that was supposed to occur on Christmas Day, she giggled and replied that she changed her mind and did not want to see me on Christmas Day since I had never spent a single Christmas with them.

I politely took the items to their automobile while the children watched, and I informed Helen Mae that since she breached the agreement, she would be responsible for the invoice. She replied, "No problem." Then the next day, Helen Mae called and informed me that she and her mother produced a preposterous story to use the toys first and then return them after Christmas.

Ironically, the concocted story failed as she informed me that the department store would not take the returns and warned her that if she did not pay as agreed, they would file felony charges against her for fraud and would request an arrest warrant. I informed Helen Mae that I would pay the invoice but advised her against engaging in this type of behavior.

Moreover, this story showed how I would make myself available to check in on the behavior of our children and now our grandchildren. My premonition regarding Helen Mae raising the grandchildren with no or little experience came to fruition. One day, when I visited them, I was approached by Lillie Mae, and she complained about the strange young man they called Roe Gary. She informed me that her mother, Helen Mae, was pushing her out to this stranger, which was exactly what Kizzy Mae did to her. But Lilli Mae was not interested in Roe Gary. In fact, she told me that he was there to see Helen Mae and not her.

One day, I heard John Wayne, Lillie Mae's son, yell out for help. "Dad, Dad, help, Dad!" I immediately ran to the back door and noticed that Roe Gary was trying to kidnap him. I ordered him to release him immediately. Keeping in mind my lack of a weapon and uncertainty about whether Roe Gary was armed, I had to use psychological tactics on him by reversing the blame and asking Roe Gray, What did John Wayne do to you?" He was baffled and released him as instructed.

We moved to a second apartment in an upscale neighborhood. One day, Helen Mae left for work with the banking industry, and my vehicle would not start. I called the bank to let Helen Mae know that she needed to come home for lunch so I could connect our batteries and jump-start my vehicle to ensure I could make it to my evening shift. But guess what? Her manager informed me that Helen Mae had called in sick and would be out for the day.

When all else had failed, I attempted to purchase another house. Even after the first home disaster, where she kept the money and subsequently purchased her a new home without me, I decided to purchase a second home this time in both our names. However, in every home we visited, there were some things that Helen Mae did not support, whether it was the ceiling being too high or the carpet being the color, etc.

In retrospect, I was always curious why my mother would tell her girlfriends that she was glad that she had six boys instead of girls. But now, after having one daughter and one stepdaughter, I am convinced that if I had boys instead of girls, my relationship with my offspring would be different because now we do not speak to each other as was the case with Kizzy Mae and Helen Mae. In other words, they are just as disrespectful to me as their mother and grandmother.

One day, I met with an insurance colleague named B. J. He informed me that during his regular canvassing and prospecting duties, he visited Walmart to meet new customers and ran into Helen Mae. When he began to talk about insurance, she informed him that her estranged husband was in the insurance business too. When she

A TEEN MARRIAGE CIRCUS

gave him my name, he informed her that I was his successor as a manager, a position he had held previously. As he continued to communicate with her, he asked what type of husband I was, and he told me that Helen Mae stated, "Abraham was an excellent husband and provider. I was just not the woman enough to keep him."

Interestingly, I can only remember three instances when Helen Mae told the truth. Firstly, she said, "You're just mad that everyone can have sex with me except you, and we are married." Secondly, she admitted, "I called the sheriff on you about child support, but regret I told you because I wanted to ruin your record." And finally, she acknowledged, "Abraham was an excellent husband and provider. I was just not the woman enough to keep him." Although we were married twice, we only lived under one roof for only fourteen days, totaling about two weeks.

Last year (2022), while I was employed with Blue Cross of Minnesota as a telesales agent, I told an older woman who was bragging about being married for fifty years that I was married twice to the same woman, Helen Mae, that lasted for two weeks combined. The older lady laughed and told her husband, who was seated nearby. After the older lady finished laughing, she told me to never tell anyone again that I was married twice to the same woman for only two weeks.

Conclusion

The cohesiveness we experienced as the Robinson family contradicted the experience that was revealed through the tumultuous relationship that I experienced with Helen Mae—a woman who had issues with her father and sibling, the one whom I would carry to her weekly psychologist appointments and whose mother, Kizzy Mae, arranged a marriage that affected the life that prevented me from achieving my dreams—a relationship that had a partner with a different background and life experience that ended the way it started and an experience that I wanted to share about my life's journey while I am available to do so.

During Helen Mae's recent visit, where she requested another opportunity to spend her last days with me and leave Fred, her estranged husband, I noticed that at the age of sixty-two, her face changed. I could no longer recognize her, resembling her mother, Kizzy Mae. But I could now see that ugly spirit that existed from the onset of this tumultuous relationship. Interestingly, all my high school friends who married girls that we all knew are still married as they made and maintained a successful relationship even to this day. Unfortunately, I was the only one to claim the title of a two-time loser!

About the Author

The author was born in the state of Alabama to his loving parents who provided a sense of purpose that paved the way for a career of opportunity and adventure. During this journey, the author earned several college degrees, including a bachelor of social and behavioral science and a master's in business administration with a focus on aviation. Also, he spent twenty-one years in the US Army and served in various duty stations worldwide. During his army tenure in the infantry corp, he taught fellow soldiers at Central College of Texas and established a platform that allowed for advancement and promotions to senior ranks because of his selfless efforts to instruct fellow soldiers during his off-duty time. Upon retirement from the army, he entered the insurance industry, earning the President's Club designation, as well as the roles of agency manager and broker.

Printed in the USA
CPSIA information can be obtained
at www.ICGtesting.com
LVHW092319050824
787261LV00001B/304